BADGERS
★ ★ ★ BY THE ★ ★ ★
NUMBERS

BADGERS

★ BY THE ★

NUMBERS

THE BEST PLAYERS AT EACH
JERSEY NUMBER IN
WISCONSIN FOOTBALL HISTORY

BY JIM POLZIN

ISBN-13: 978-0-97987-29-8-3
ISBN-10: 0-97987-29-8-7

Cover and book design by Brandon Raygo
Contributions by Adam Mertz
Special thanks to Ken Miller, Gary Neuenschwander, Lisa Nelson,
Amy Mertz, Mario Puig and Nate Carey

This book is available in quantity at special discounts for your group or
organization. For further information, contact:
KCI Sports Publishing
3340 Whiting Avenue
Suite 5
Stevens Point, WI 54481
(217)-766-3390 Fax (715) 344-8833

Photos courtesy of the Wisconsin State Journal, Madison Capital Times, and
the University of Wisconsin athletic department.

THE ROSTER ★ ★ ★

#	Name	#	Name	#	Name
1	Brandon Williams	34	Pat Harder	67	Dan Buenning
2	Jamar Fletcher	35	Alan Ameche	68	Terry Stieve
3	Lee Evans	36	Earl Girard	69	Derek Engler
4	Michael Jones	37	Cecil Martin	70	Dennis Lick
5	Brooks Bollinger	38	Nate Odomes	71	Dave Suminski
6	Jack Ikegwuonu	39	Matt VandenBoom	72	Joe Thomas
7	John Stocco	40	Elroy Hirsch	73	Dan Lanphear
8	Jason Doering	41	Milo Lubratovich	74	Tom Burke
9	Travis Beckum	42	Tarek Saleh	75	Chris McIntosh
10	Mike Samuel	43	Aaron Stecker	76	Bill Gregory
11	Ed Withers	44	Donnel Thompson	77	Wendell Bryant
12	Randy Wright	45	Nick Greisen	78	Ross Kolodziej
13	Carl McCullough	46	Jeff Mack	79	Aaron Gibson
14	Dave Crossen	47	Ed Jankowski	80	Dave Schreiner
15	Ron Vander Kelen	48	Pete Monty	81	Hal Faverty
16	Chris Ghidorzi	49	Harold Rebholz	82	Tony Simmons
17	Allen Langford	50	Tim Krumrie	83	Allan Shafer
18	Jim Leonhard	51	Mike Webster	84	Donald Hayes
19	Danny Lewis	52	Cory Raymer	85	Bryan Jurewicz
20	Ed Crofoot	53	Robert Wilson	86	Ron Leafblad
21	Rufus Ferguson	54	Gary Messner	87	Al Toon
22	Troy Vincent	55	Chad Yocum	88	Pat Richter
23	Joe Armentrout	56	Frank Molinaro	89	Albert Hannah
24	Neovia Greyer	57	Ken Bowman	90	Don Voss
25	Ira Matthews	58	Joe Panos	91	Don Davey
26	Billy Marek	59	Mario Pacetti	92	Carlos Fowler
27	John Coatta	60	Darryl Sims	93	Frederick Gage
28	Dale Hackbart	61	Mike Lorenz	94	Ken DeBauche
29	Richard Johnson	62	Paul Gruber	95	Tim Jordan
30	Larry Canada	63	Joe Rudolph	96	John Favret
31	David Greenwood	64	Ken Currier	97	Mike Allen
32	Mark Montgomery	65	Jamie Vanderveldt	98	Yusef Burgess
33	Ron Dayne	66	Mike Thompson	99	Rick Graf

FOREWORD

It was only a matter of time until we were to be served up a book that is this unique.

With all the technology that is available today, I am continually amazed as to the multiplicity of ways statistics can be sliced and diced. It becomes a bit overwhelming at times and quite frankly irrelevant and boring.

Not so with *Badgers By the Numbers*.

This book is fascinating because the reader can relate to football players as real people. We have the opportunity to test our memory and recall all of our favorites. Often times that affection to a particular player has nothing to do with his stats. Maybe the player gave you an autograph or came to school to talk to you when you were a kid. Whatever the reason, a special bond develops which remains with us throughout our childhood, and in some cases, our entire life.

While this book is exclusively dedicated to the Badgers, some readers will logically make the leap to the Big Ten or even include the pro ranks. Not only is it a good read but the book can evolve into a "game" of sorts. Suffice it to say that it is a book that will not be without controversy — and therein lies the full enjoyment of the work.

Having had the pleasure of being asked to weigh in on who I thought were the top performers at each number, you'll find, as I did, a few surprises along the way. What jumped out to me was that many of the players that I recall and believed were deserving of mention wore the same number as a player that was ultimately selected.

Among the voters there was occasional disagreement and I believe that is understandable, depending on how old they were and how long they had followed the Badgers. For the public in general, I

believe they would be more likely to connect with more recent players. There is no doubt that the proliferation of media types and the number of outlets has an impact on how the list was compiled, and how it will be viewed.

One other observation I made is that it appears that many so-called "top" players seemed to gravitate to certain numbers, whether it be by coincidence or the desire of someone on the staff wanting them to wear a particular number. And, of course, as a first-year varsity player you have to be lucky enough to have your "favorite" number available, and not already assigned to an upperclassman. I know in my case when I was given a jersey it was No. 88, and as far as I know, it was purely luck of the draw. But maybe someone wanted me to wear that number.

Similarly, there are a few numbers that have had very little usage by players that are easily recognized and you were tempted to use that number for a player who may have been justifiably placed behind an obvious choice.

I know one thing for sure: This would have been a project that the late Jim Mott and Tom Butler would have loved. Mott, the longtime UW sports information director, and Butler, the legendary *Wisconsin State Journal* reporter, could have selected a player at every number and it's doubtful they would have been second-guessed.

But with Jim and Tom gone, have at it, have some fun. Come up with your own list. Maybe you can even make up a "number" fantasy football team!

Good luck, and Go Badgers!

–Pat Richter

★ ★ ★ ★ ★ ★ ★ ★ ★ ★ ★ ★ ★ INTRODUCTION ★ ★ ★ ★ ★ ★ ★ ★ ★ ★ ★ ★ ★

Tom Butler made a good point about all-time lists. "Let's face it," the long-time sports writer for the *Wisconsin State Journal* once wrote, "all-time teams are designed to create controversy."

I promise that wasn't the idea behind putting together an All-Time Roster for the University of Wisconsin football program based on the best player at each jersey number.

This idea was hatched late in the 2007 season, right around the time Ron Dayne's No. 33 jersey was retired by UW that November. The following weekend, I was hanging out with some buddies in Minnesota the night before the Badgers played the Gophers, and we began a list of the best players at each jersey number.

We got through the first three numbers -- Brandon Williams at No. 1, Jamar Fletcher at No. 2, Lee Evans at No. 3 -- before moving on to another subject, probably because we were stumped at No. 4.

More than a year later, the list was finally completed and published in *The Capital Times*.

While the concept wasn't created to stir up controversy, as Butler wrote, we realize that our choices will spawn debate. And that's good. In fact, we encourage it. Take a look at the back of this book, where we list the players who were considered for this honor, and let us know where we

went wrong.

Here's how we came up with the list:

The first step was figuring out candidates at each number. To do that, we entered rosters from the 1920s -- when numbers first appeared on the back of jerseys -- to the present into a sortable database that is accessible online at Madison.com sports.

We formed a panel that includes UW officials along with current and former media members. We indicated our tentative choice for a majority of the numbers, but invited our panelists to select another player if they chose. In some cases -- like Mike Samuel beating out our initial choice, All-American kicker Taylor Mehlhaff at No. 10 -- changes were made based on overwhelming feedback from the panel. (*The State Journal's* Butler, by the way, would have been an ideal member on this panel, but he passed away in June 2008.)

Note that we decided to disqualify current players from consideration.

Special thanks to Justin Doherty, Brian Lucas and Rudy Nigl in UW's athletic communications department for all of their help with this project. I spent a great deal of time gathering photos in the archives room on the second floor of Kellner Hall, but the process would have taken much longer if Doherty and his staff weren't so organized.

With that, we present our list. Debate away. But most of all, enjoy.

The school's all-time leader in receptions (202) and kickoff return yards (2,349), Williams was a model of consistency during his time at UW. He had 52 receptions as a freshman, 49 as a sophomore, 42 as a junior and 59 as a senior, when he led the Big Ten in receiving yards and became only the second player in program history to top the 1,000-yard mark in a single season. Williams was named a second-team All-American by the Associated Press that season and was drafted in the third round by the San Francisco 49ers the following spring. He played two seasons in the NFL and is still pursuing a pro career. "He's such a great competitor," UW quarterback John Stocco told *The Capital Times* during Williams' senior season in 2005. "I love having that guy out there, because he's going to do everything in his power to make a big play. And he wants the ball so bad."

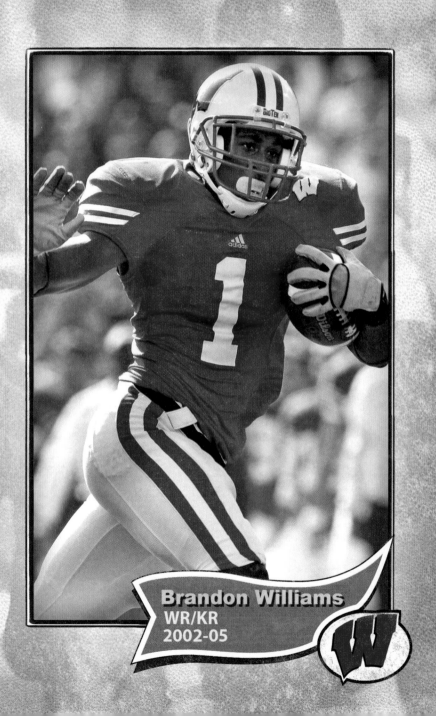

Brandon Williams
WR/KR
2002-05

One of the greatest playmakers in program history and also one of its biggest talkers. Fletcher oozed with confidence, at times asking the coaching staff to be matched up with the opponent's top wide receiver. "If your mouth writes a check," former Badgers coach Barry Alvarez warned Fletcher, stealing a line from his old boss, Lou Holtz, "your fanny better be able to cash it." Fletcher backed up his words. He had seven interceptions in each of his three seasons – he's tied with Jim Leonhard as the program's career leader in picks – and returned five of them for touchdowns. After winning the Thorpe Award, given to the top defensive back in the nation, and being named the Big Ten's Defensive Player of the Year in 2000, Fletcher chose to skip his senior season at UW and head to the NFL. He was a first-round pick of the Miami Dolphins and completed his eighth professional season in 2008.

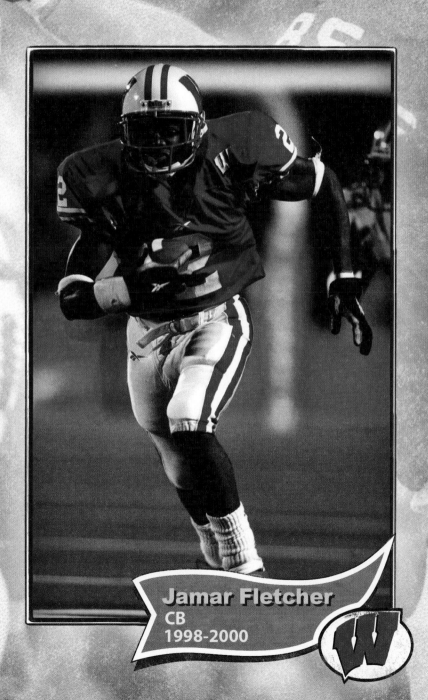

Jamar Fletcher
CB
1998-2000

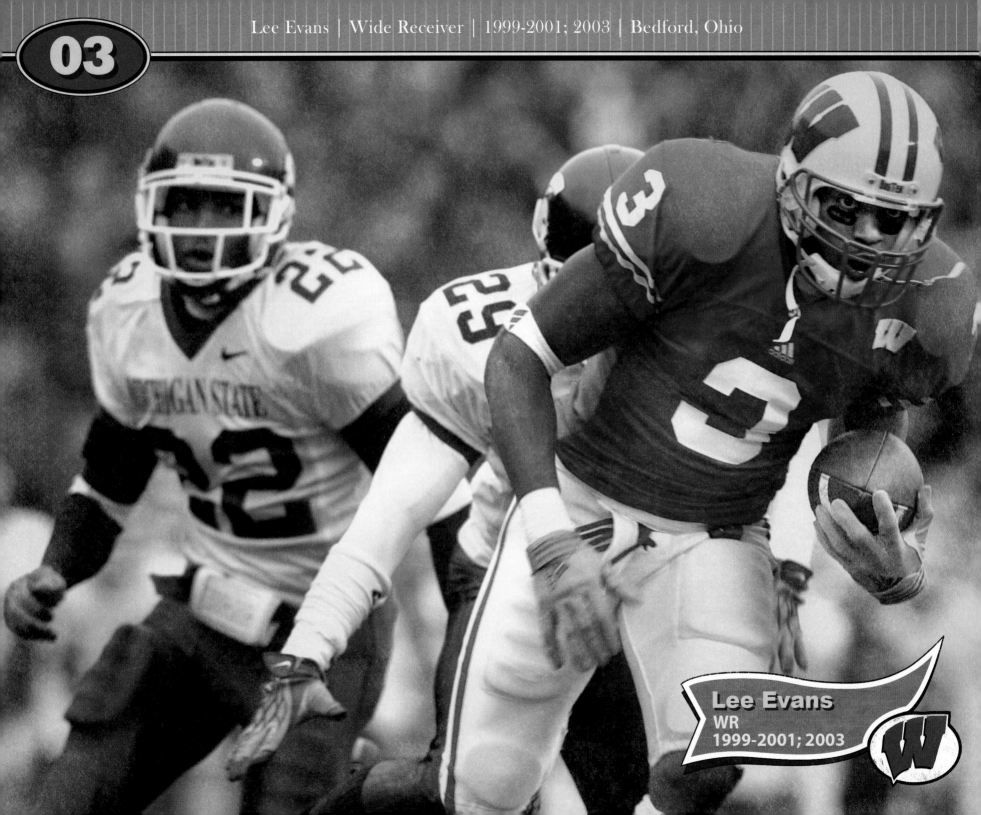

03

Lee Evans
WR
1999-2001; 2003

Part of Lee Evans' "How I Spent My Summer Vacation" tale involves a trip to Minneapolis, of all places.

There, he spent a few days training with some of the best wide receivers in the NFL, past and present, on the University of Minnesota campus.

Evans, who has five NFL seasons under his belt, didn't hesitate when he was invited to the offseason receivers camp orchestrated by Arizona Cardinals star and Minneapolis native Larry Fitzgerald. Like Evans, Fitzgerald was a first-round selection in the 2004 NFL Draft.

Instructors at the sessions, which were also attended by Green Bay Packers standout Greg Jennings, included former NFL greats Jerry Rice and Cris Carter.

"It was nice to get out and work with those guys," said Evans, who has registered two 1,000-yard seasons, including a breakout campaign in 2006 in which he had 82 receptions for 1,292 yards and eight touchdowns. "It was a chance to get out and do something different and see what other guys are doing. You could pick other guys' brains."

Evans, who signed a four-year, $37.25 million contract extension in 2008 and is looking forward to working with new teammate Terrell Owens this season, could have given a tutorial on getting yardage in huge chunks. He's had six touchdowns of 70 or more yards during his career – nobody in the NFL has more this decade – and averaged 16.1 yards per reception last season, which ranked fourth among players with 60 or more catches.

None of that surprises Evans' former wide receivers coach, Henry Mason, who has been watching from afar since Evans' record-breaking career at UW.

"It's interesting, he'll make a play and they'll go on and on about the

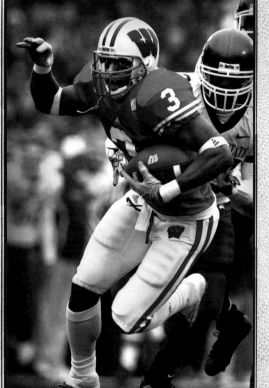

great play he just made," said Mason, now UW's director of player personnel. "But we around here have seen it over and over again. It doesn't surprise us."

Nobody quite knew what to expect from Evans, who followed former high school teammate Chris Chambers to Madison, when he arrived at UW in 1999. Evans didn't put up huge numbers during his prep career – his team operated out of the Wing-T offense – and therefore was a bit of an unknown on the recruiting front.

It didn't take long for Evans to prove he belonged, however.

"You had a pretty good idea two or three days into (training) camp by watching him compete and seeing how well he picked things up," Mason said. "Certainly there was a learning curve, but you knew he had the skills to be a good player and that he was going to be smart enough to learn what he needed to learn."

Still, nobody could have seen Evans putting up the numbers he did in a UW program that liked to pound the ball on the ground. The Badgers were in the midst of 10 consecutive seasons with a 1,000-yard rusher from 1993-2002.

Evans recorded the first 1,000-yard receiving season in UW history in 2001, when he finished with 75 receptions for 1,545 yards and was named a first-team All-American. Two seasons later – he sat out the 2002 campaign after he injured his knee in the spring game – Evans closed his career in style with 64 receptions for 1,213 yards and 13 touchdowns.

"The one thing that I tried to do was work hard and try to earn the respect of my coaches and my teammates," said Evans, UW's all-time leader in receiving yards (3,468) and TD receptions (27). "Once I did that, they weren't opposed to putting the ball in my hands."

Jones made an impact right away at UW. He led the Badgers in receiving in 1981, when he was named to *Football News'* Freshman All-American team. He ranks eighth all-time at UW in touchdown receptions (12) and 14th in receiving yards (1,266). Jones was also dangerous as a return man; he's one of just four players in program history with a 100-yard kickoff return.

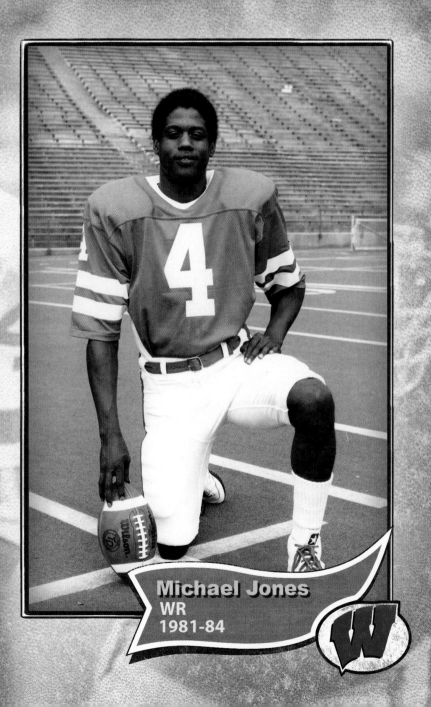

Michael Jones
WR
1981-84

Brooks Bollinger
QB
1999-2002

There are plenty of numbers that made Bollinger stand out during his four seasons as UW's starting quarterback. He finished his career with 5,627 passing yards and 38 touchdown passes; both marks are No. 3 all-time at UW. He also is tied for sixth with 26 career rushing touchdowns. But the number he was most proud of was 30: the tally of UW wins in games he started. The bookmarks of that career are both special: overcoming a 17-point deficit in a 42-17 victory at 12th-ranked Ohio State in 1999 in his first start, which snapped a two-game Badgers losing streak and commenced a march to a second straight Rose Bowl victory, and coming from behind to beat Colorado in overtime in the 2002 Alamo Bowl, the final game of Bollinger's career. He has played five seasons in the NFL, including a nine-game stint as the New York Jets' starter in 2005.

Lightly recruited out of Madison Memorial High School, Ikegwuonu developed into a shut-down cornerback. A two-time first-team All-Big Ten performer, he started 29 games in three seasons before passing up his final year of eligibility to enter the NFL Draft. Ikegwuonu finished his career with six interceptions, including three in 2005, when he was named honorable mention freshman All-American by *The Sporting News*. Ikegwuonu was selected in the fourth round of the 2008 NFL Draft after sustaining a knee injury leading up to the draft; he spent the 2008 season on injured reserve.

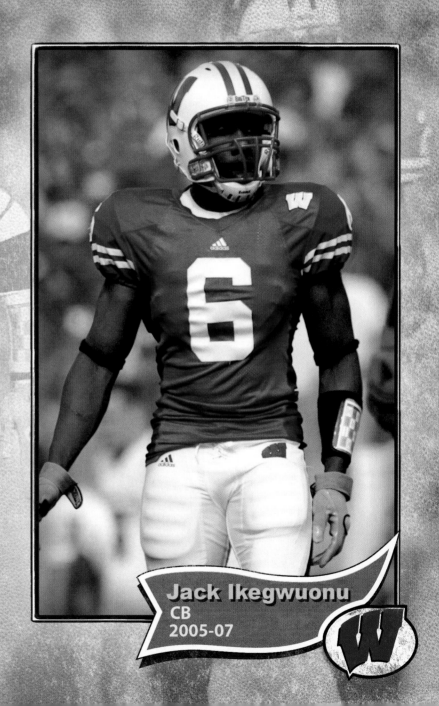

Jack Ikegwuonu
CB
2005-07

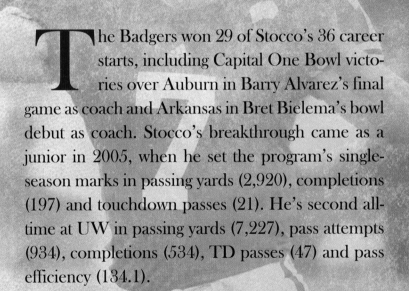

John Stocco
QB
2003-06

The Badgers won 29 of Stocco's 36 career starts, including Capital One Bowl victories over Auburn in Barry Alvarez's final game as coach and Arkansas in Bret Bielema's bowl debut as coach. Stocco's breakthrough came as a junior in 2005, when he set the program's single-season marks in passing yards (2,920), completions (197) and touchdown passes (21). He's second all-time at UW in passing yards (7,227), pass attempts (934), completions (534), TD passes (47) and pass efficiency (134.1).

One of UW's great walk-on stories, Doering was a starter on teams that won back-to-back Big Ten and Rose Bowl championships in 1998 and '99. Not only did Doering earn a scholarship during his time with the Badgers, he was twice named captain and left his mark as a ferocious hitter and sound tackler. His 338 tackles are 12th all-time at UW; the only UW defensive backs with more career stops are Greg Thomas (359) and Reggie Holt (344). Doering was selected by Indianapolis Colts in the sixth round of the 2001 NFL Draft and played from 2001-03.

Jason Doering
S
1997-2000

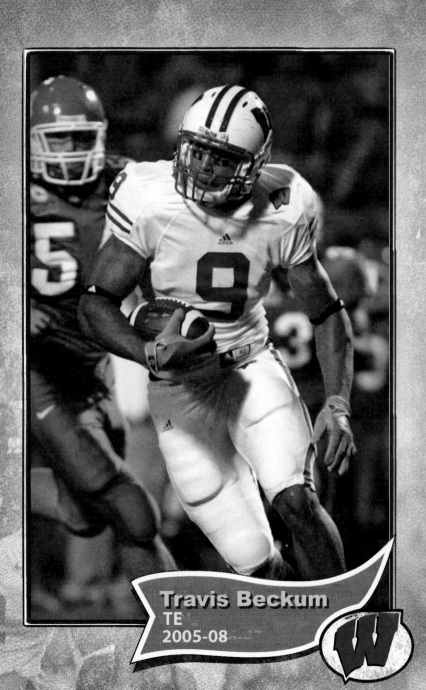

Travis Beckum
TE
2005-08

Beckum arrived at UW as a highly decorated recruit and was expected to make an immediate impact on the defensive side of the ball. He didn't, but was moved to offense after his first season and re-wrote the record book as a tight end. He finished his career third at UW in career receptions (159) and receiving yards (2,149) despite missing half of his senior season with a broken leg. Beckum was a first-team All-American as a junior in 2007, when he led all tight ends nationally and tied the school's single-season record with 75 receptions. He's one of two Badgers to have 10 or more receptions in a game twice in his career. Beckum was selected in the third round of the 2009 NFL Draft by the New York Giants.

Numbers don't begin to define Samuel's worth to the program, although he's fifth in career passing yards (4,989), sixth in touchdown passes (24) and 10th in rushing touchdowns (23). What stood out about Samuel was his toughness and winning mentality. A three-year starter in the same backfield as Heisman Trophy winner and all-time college football leading rusher Ron Dayne, Samuel capped off his career by helping the Badgers win a Big Ten championship in 1998 and a victory over highly favored UCLA in the 1999 Rose Bowl.

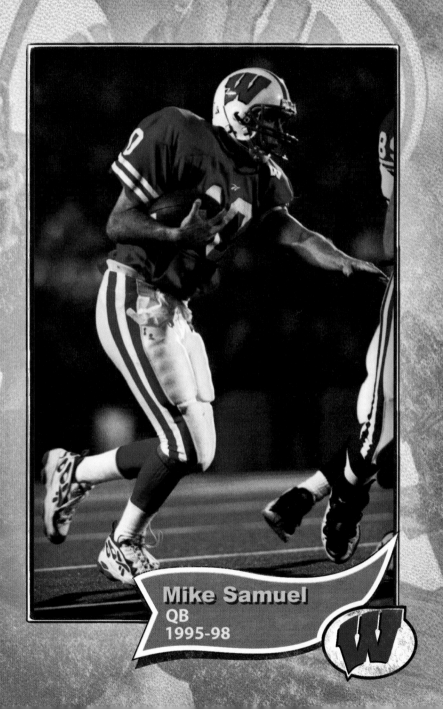

Mike Samuel
QB
1995-98

Ed Withers
DB
1949-51

Withers made history in 1950 when he became the Badgers' first African-American to earn All-America honors in football. He didn't stop there, earning All-America honors the next season as well. A member of UW's famed "Hard Rocks" defensive unit in 1951, Withers finished his career with eight interceptions, including three in a game against Iowa in 1950. A Memphis, Tenn., native, Withers migrated north and attended Madison Central High School. His studies were interrupted by military service, as he was drafted into the Army and spent nearly two years in Japan and Korea before returning to earn his diploma. As a result, Withers was 24 when he completed college. When he died in 1975, he remained UW's only black All-American. Withers was selected by the Green Bay Packers in the 30th round of the 1951 NFL Draft but never played for the team.

12

Randy Wright
QB
1981-83

A transfer from Notre Dame, Wright became the first UW player to pass for more than 2,000 yards in a season in 1982, when he was named UW's MVP. Wright ranks fourth all-time at UW in passing yards (5,003) and is tied for third in touchdown passes (38). He also holds the program's fourth- and fifth-best single-season passing yardage totals. Wright was selected by the Green Bay Packers in the sixth round of the 1984 NFL Draft and played from 1984-88.

13

McCullough is 10th all-time at UW with 2,111 rushing yards, almost half of which (1,038) came during his sophomore season in 1995. Who knows how many yards McCullough would have rushed for during his career had it not been for the arrival of Ron Dayne, who supplanted McCullough in the starting lineup early in the 1996 season? Despite being a backup, McCullough was named a captain as a senior in 1997. He had one final signature moment; while filling in for the injured Dayne, he powered for 106 yards on 20 carries against top-ranked Michigan in a hard-fought 26-16 loss at Camp Randall on Nov. 15, 1997.

Carl McCullough
RB
1993; 1995-97

Pound for pound, Crossen is one of the toughest players to wear a UW uniform. He earned second-team All-Big Ten honors as a sophomore, despite weighing just 189 pounds. Crossen is tied for fourth all-time at UW with 427 tackles. He holds the school record with 28 tackles in a game against Purdue in 1977. He was named the Badgers' MVP that season. Crossen had 23 or more tackles in a game four times during his career and led UW in tackles as a junior and senior.

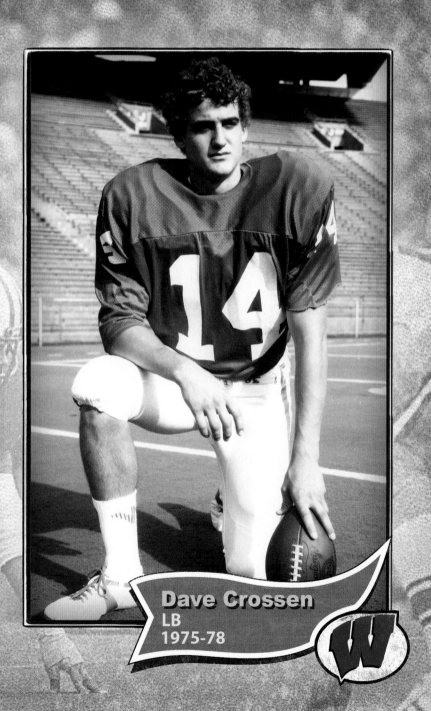

Dave Crossen
LB
1975-78

* *

TWO HUNDRED
* * * TWENTY ONE * * *

Through 2008, 221 University of Wisconsin football players had gone on to professional careers. Of that number, 24 were drafted in the first round. Two — Elroy "Crazylegs" Hirsch and Mike Webster — are in the Pro Football Hall of Fame.

* *

Ron Vander Kelen
QB
1962

During his time in the admissions department at the Minnesota School of Business late in his professional career, Ron Vander Kelen often tried to inspire students with the story of how he beat the odds.

Not once during those conversations did Vander Kelen discuss his rapid rise from obscurity to star quarterback in 1962. There was no mention of how Vander Kelen, a first-year starter, was named a first-team All-Big Ten pick after leading the league in passing yards that season.

And unless they were college football history buffs – or the descendants of longtime Badgers fans – those students left the room with no clue that Vander Kelen threw for 401 yards during a 42-37 loss to USC in the 1963 Rose Bowl, still considered one of the greatest games in the bowl's storied history.

Instead, Vander Kelen chose to focus on the important details. Like how, after sitting out the 1961 season because of academic issues, he got his act together and ended up leaving UW with a diploma.

"I graduated, and that was not easy with all the goofing off that I did in '59 and '60 and getting some low grades," Vander Kelen said. "I worked pretty darn hard and I'm proud of myself for doing that."

Vander Kelen can chuckle now when telling the story. Back then, it was no laughing matter.

"The easiest thing," Vander Kelen said, "would have been to just say, 'The heck with it,' and walk away."

Had he done that, Vander Kelen never would have ended up in admissions, where he had the opportunity to help point students in the right direction prior to retiring in 2007.

Whether it was conversations with prospective students or students who were struggling to stay in school, Vander Kelen would often hear the phrase, "I can't do this."

His response?

"Well, I had the history of saying that myself. But I did the best I could.

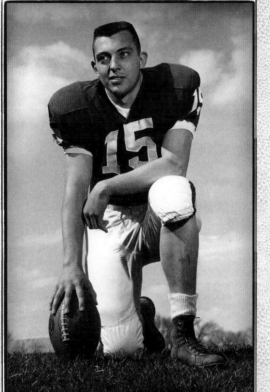

And if you get knocked down, get up, dust yourself off and move forward."

Vander Kelen has a videotape of the 1963 Rose Bowl, but he says he hasn't watched it in about 20 years. Every once in a while, he says, it will dawn on him just how unbelievable it was that he played a major role on that great team.

Besides missing the prior season with academic struggles, Vander Kelen had sat out the 1960 season with a knee injury. He was a third-stringer as a sophomore in 1959, when Dale Hackbart was the starter and led the Badgers to the Rose Bowl. (And had Ron Miller, the starter in 1961, been granted an extra year of eligibility after missing a season due to injury, he likely would have remained at the helm of that vaunted Badgers team.)

Heck, Vander Kelen remembers being one of 13 quarterbacks on the roster when he arrived in 1958 and played on the freshman team.

"I try not to live in the past, but I've been fortunate enough to have some really great memories," he said. "I'm never going to forget all those wonderful things that happened to me, but I just keep trying to move on with my life."

After finishing his UW career, Vander Kelen played five seasons with the Minnesota Vikings. From there, he went on to a successful business career in advertising and marketing before going into education.

Vander Kelen, who lives near Minneapolis, retired in 2007 but still does part-time work for a company that reviews No Child Left Behind tests.

"I'll never forget what Milt Bruhn and the coaching staff did for me," said Vander Kelen, who turns 70 in November 2009. "They gave me the break of my lifetime. If it wasn't for that, where would I be today? And what would I be today?

"I don't even want to think about where I might have been. But it would not be the person that I am today."

16

Chris Ghidorzi
LB
1996-99

Ghidorzi started on UW teams that won back-to-back Big Ten and Rose Bowl titles. As a senior in 1999, he was a team captain and led the team in tackles with 115. A year earlier, he finished second in tackles for a unit that allowed the fewest points per game nationally. A three-time Academic All-Big Ten performer, Ghidorzi was named UW's Ivan Williamson Scholastic Award winner in 1999.

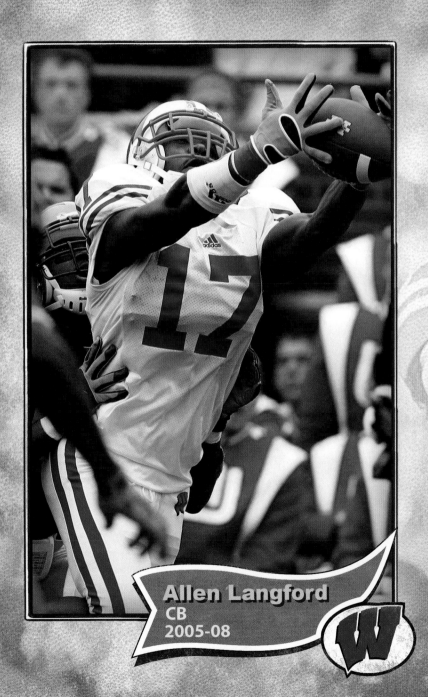

Allen Langford
CB
2005-08

Though he wasn't the fastest cornerback, Langford made up for it with meticulous preparation and solid technique. He was a fixture in UW's lineup for four seasons, finishing with 41 career starts. He ended his career with a bang; after sustaining a torn ACL in his knee late in his junior season, Langford came back strong in 2008 and was named first-team All-Big Ten and the Badgers' MVP.

The Jim Leonhard story just kept getting better during his time with the Badgers. He arrived as a walk-on from a small town in northwestern Wisconsin and played on special teams as a true freshman. A year later, he led the nation and tied a Big Ten record with 11 interceptions. By the time he left UW, the diminutive Leonhard -- who stands just 5-foot-8 and weighed 186 pounds as a collegian -- was a three-time All-American and first-team All-Big Ten choice. His name is plastered all over UW's record books. He's the program's all-time leader in punt return yards with 1,347 and is tied with Jamar Fletcher for the all-time interceptions lead with 21. An undrafted free agent, Leonhard played three seasons with the Buffalo Bills and one with the Baltimore Ravens before joining the New York Jets as a free agent following the 2008 season.

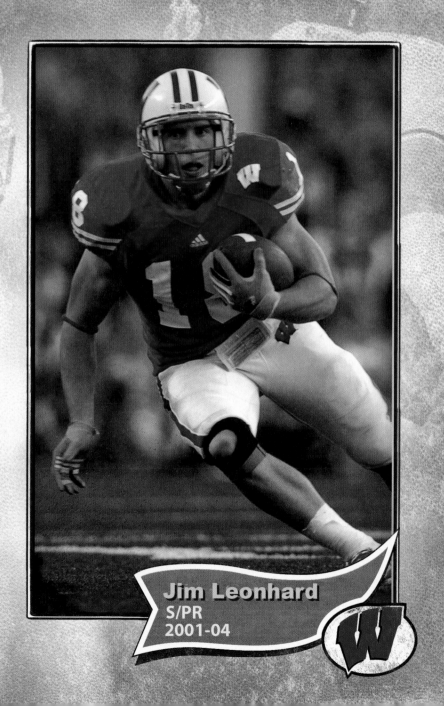

Jim Leonhard
S/PR
2001-04

19

When Lewis led the Badgers with 611 rushing yards in 1957 – averaging 6.4 yards per carry in the process – the only UW player who had rushed for more yards in a single season up to that point was Alan Ameche. Lewis also led the team in rushing the previous season and was a dangerous receiving threat out of the backfield. He was drafted in the sixth round of the 1958 NFL Draft and played nine seasons in the league with the Detroit Lions, Washington Redskins and New York Giants.

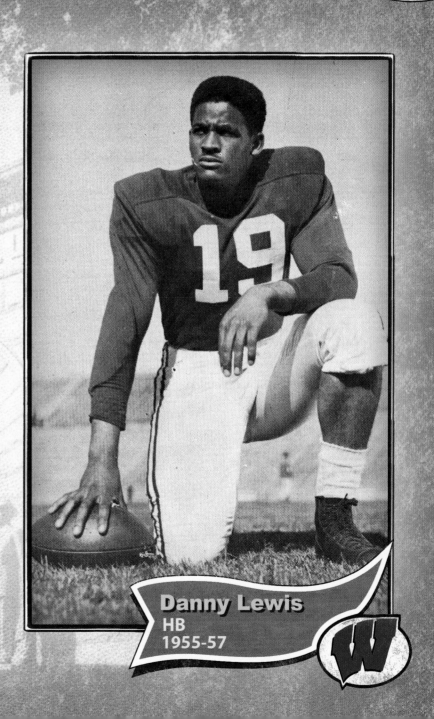

Danny Lewis
HB
1955-57

Nicknamed "Toad," Crofoot—who worked his way into the lineup at quarterback as a sophomore under Hall of Fame coach George Little — was named first-team All-Big Ten in 1927. He also served as a captain for the Badgers that season. UW went 15-7-2 during Crofoot's three seasons, including a stretch of nine games in which the Badgers were not defeated (7-0-2). Alas, he was unable to end a familiar hex for the UW football program, with Wisconsin shut out in all three showdowns against Michigan during his career, extending a winless streak against the Wolverines to 28 years. "Crofoot has football brains," read the Associated Press season preview of the 1927 Badgers. "He runs his team with snap and dash and keeps the spirit of the eleven at a high ebb with his great amount of fire and fight. He is a proverbial chatterbox from the background position and should make a capable leader."

Ed Crofoot
HB
1925-27

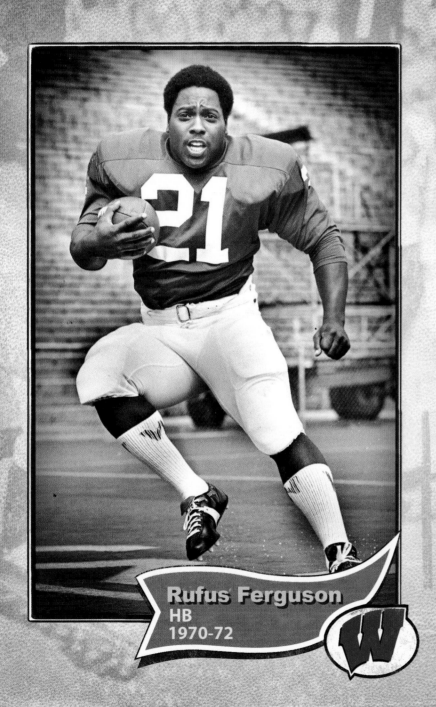

Rufus Ferguson
HB
1970-72

Ferguson arrived at UW with a nickname – "The Roadrunner" – from his exploits as base stealer during his prep baseball career. His end zone dances were just as exciting as his runs; that was no small feat considering how productive the 5-foot-6 Ferguson was during his career, which helped resurrect a Badgers program that snapped a 23-game winless streak the year before he set foot on campus. He set a UW record with 1,222 rushing yards in 1971 and followed that up with 1,004 yards as a senior. Ferguson still ranks ninth all-time at UW with 2,814 yards and is tied for sixth with 26 rushing touchdowns. Ferguson was recognized at a banquet following his senior season, with then-athletic director Elroy Hirsch thanking him "for all the excitement and thrills, not to mention all the fannies you put in the seats."

Troy Vincent
CB
1988-91

Troy Vincent simply moved on to the next play, just as if he had been beaten for a 70-yard touchdown in the Super Bowl.

That's one way of looking at how Vincent responded to being passed over for the post of executive director of the NFL Players Association in March 2009. DeMaurice Smith was selected as union head over Vincent, the NFLPA's president from 2004-08, in a vote by player representatives from each of the league's 32 teams.

When the shock wore off, Vincent turned his focus to his other business interests. He serves as the managing director for a business consulting firm and as the CEO for Troy Vincent Development and Construction, which deals in residential and commercial real estate.

"Basically, I gave up my life for five or six months, just preparing to take that post," said Vincent, an All-Pro cornerback during his 15-year career in the NFL. "That was my goal, to win and succeed. I fell short. They wanted to go in a different direction, and all I did was close that chapter of my life and move on and say that was not in God's plan for me."

Vincent called it a "wonderful experience," even though it turned controversial in the final months.

Some reports questioned his outside business interests. Another report revealed accusations from some inside the NFLPA that he had disclosed confidential information on player agents in an e-mail to a business partner.

Vincent admits he felt a bit like a politician. But quitting didn't enter his mind, even when things got nasty.

"During the whole process, I was thankful," he said. "At the end of the day, I was representing the people of Wisconsin, the University of Wisconsin and everyone else that had been associated with me.

"I wanted to make sure when I walked away, win or lose, I walked away proudly. And that the people – coach (Barry Alvarez), Pat Richter – could say, 'That was a job well done. One of ours was being considered there.' "

Alvarez couldn't be prouder of the man Vincent has become. Alvarez still remembers his first few meetings with Vincent after taking over as UW's coach in 1990.

"He wasn't confident at all," Alvarez said. "We had to convince him he was good."

He was good, all right. Vincent went on to become the Big Ten's co-defensive player of the year and a first-team All-American as a senior in 1991. A few months later, the Miami Dolphins made him the seventh overall selection of the NFL Draft.

Vincent was selected to five Pro Bowls during his NFL career and recently was named to ESPN.com's all-decade team for the 1990s.

Vincent is proud to be a Badger, even though he almost wasn't one.

"I went there for a visit and I knew I wasn't going there," Vincent said of UW, which was going nowhere at the time under the direction of Don Morton. "It was cold, there was nothing to do, at the time they were 3-8. There was no need for me to really even consider that."

When Vincent told his mother he was going to Syracuse, she shook her head. "No, you're not," she told him. Then she told him he was going to Wisconsin.

"It was the best decision," Vincent said. "It helped me bring a bunch of balance into my life, meeting different people from different parts of the world. My experience was one that I will cherish for a lifetime."

23

The versatile Armentrout was effective as a blocker, ball-carrier and pass-catcher out of the backfield. A two-time offensive MVP for the Badgers, Armentrout was captain of the 1986 team. He finished his career with 1,576 rushing yards – 20th all-time at UW – and 68 receptions. He was also an All-Big Ten center fielder in baseball. Armentrout was drafted in the ninth round of the 1987 NFL Draft by the Tampa Bay Buccaneers.

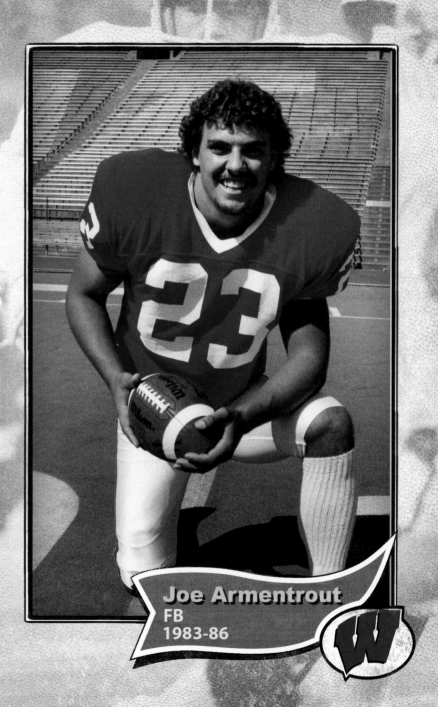

Joe Armentrout
FB
1983-86

Neovia Greyer
DB
1969-71

Greyer had 18 interceptions, tied for third all-time at UW. One of those came in the final minute of a 23-17 victory over Iowa in 1969 that ended a 23-game winless streak (0-22-1) that dated to the start of the 1967 season. Greyer's nine interceptions in 1970 were the most in a single season until Jim Leonhard (11) eclipsed the mark more than three decades later. Greyer was selected in the 16th round of the 1972 NFL Draft by the New York Giants.

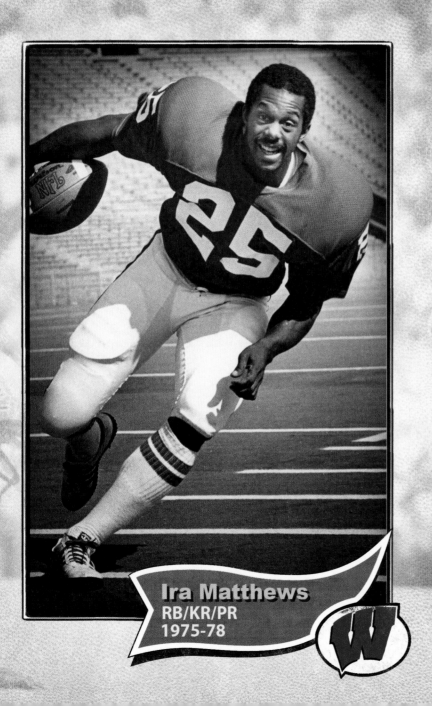

Ira Matthews
RB/KR/PR
1975-78

Arguably the most dangerous return man in UW history, Matthews led the nation in kickoff return average (29.6) in 1976 and punt return average (16.9) in 1978. His four punt return touchdowns are the most in program history and his two kickoff return touchdowns are tied for the most. Matthews is one of four players in school history with a 100-yard kickoff return. He also led the team in rushing as a senior. Matthews was selected by Oakland in the sixth round of the 1979 NFL Draft and played three seasons with the Raiders.

26

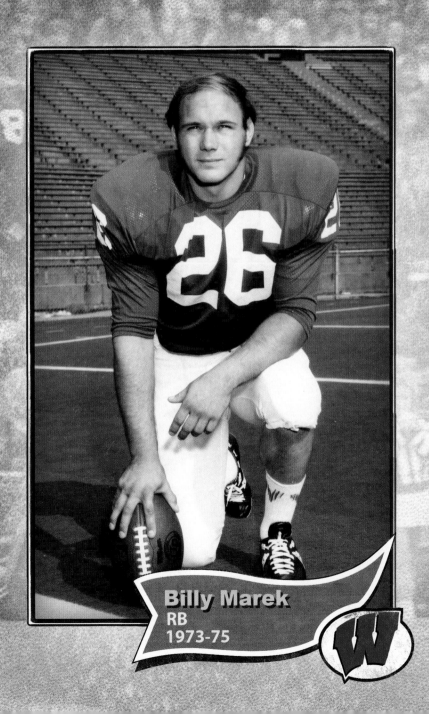

Billy Marek
RB
1973-75

Marek was the Badgers' career rushing leader for more than two decades before Ron Dayne passed him in 1998. Marek, who played just three seasons, now stands fourth all-time with 3,709 rushing yards, trailing Dayne, Anthony Davis and P.J. Hill. He's also tied for second all-time at UW with 44 touchdowns and tied for third in scoring with 278 points. A three-time first-team All-Big Ten selection, Marek was a second-team AP All-American in 1974.

Coatta was the first Big Ten quarterback to throw for more than 1,000 yards in a season. He led the league in passing in 1950 and '51, earning first-team All-Big Ten honors as a senior. Coatta went on to become UW's head coach from 1967-69, although he struggled mightily; the Badgers were 3-26-1 during the Coatta era, including a 23-game winless stretch.

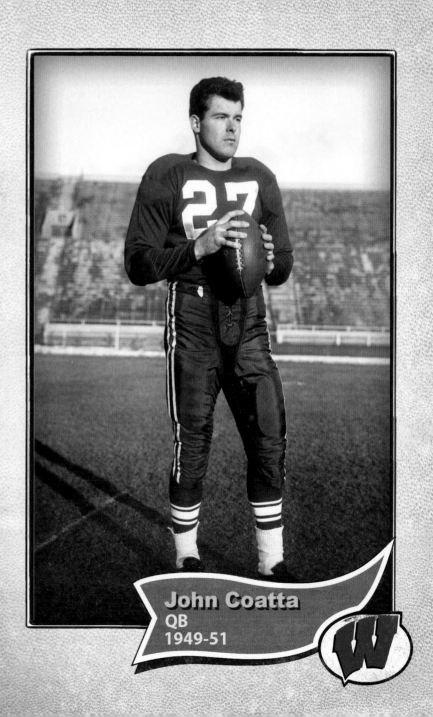

John Coatta
QB
1949-51

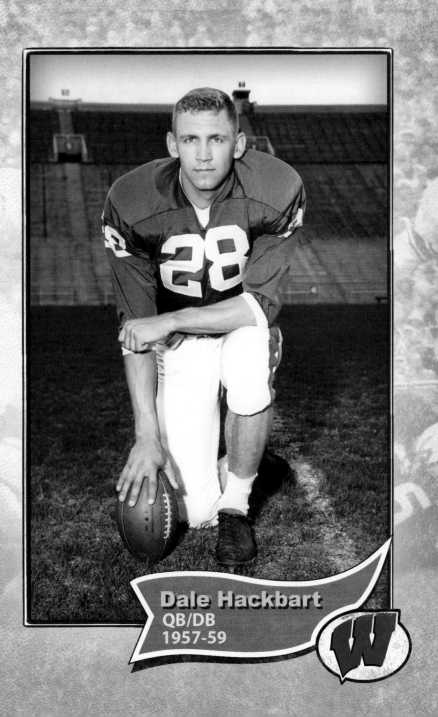

Hackbart could do it all. He had seven interceptions in 1958; only two players in UW history have had more in a single season. The following season, Hackbart was a first-team All-Big Ten selection at quarterback for the Rose Bowl-bound Badgers after leading the league in total offensive yards and leading Wisconsin in rushing. A first-team Academic All-American, Hackbart was selected by the Green Bay Packers in the fifth round of 1960 NFL Draft. He played with five teams over a 12-year career.

Dale Hackbart
QB/DB
1957-59

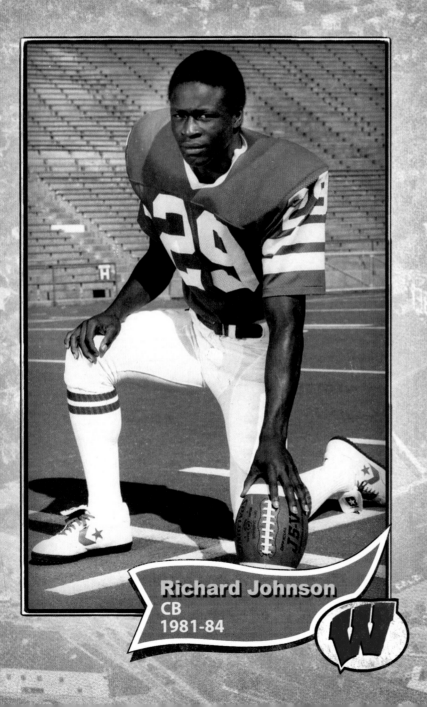

Richard Johnson
CB
1981-84

N obody at UW was better at blocking kicks. Johnson had a school-record six blocked kicks in 1984 – including three in a game against Missouri – and finished his career with nine. Nobody else at UW has more than five. Johnson was an All-American as a senior and was selected 11th overall by Houston in the NFL Draft the following spring. He played eight seasons with the Oilers.

Larry Canada
FB
1973-76

After clearing space for tailback Billy Marek in 1975, Canada took over as UW's featured back as a senior and led the team with 996 rushing yards. He only lost three yards on 221 carries that season. Canada went on to play three seasons with the Denver Broncos and three more in the United States Football League with the Denver Gold and Chicago Blitz.

31

A two-time first-team All-Big Ten selection, Greenwood finished his career with 10 interceptions. He was also an accomplished track and field athlete at UW; he claimed a Big Ten outdoor title in the high jump. Greenwood was the first pick in the inaugural United States Football League draft. He played three seasons in the USFL – helping the Michigan Panthers win the title in 1983, the league's first season of existence – and three more in the NFL, including one with the Green Bay Packers in 1986.

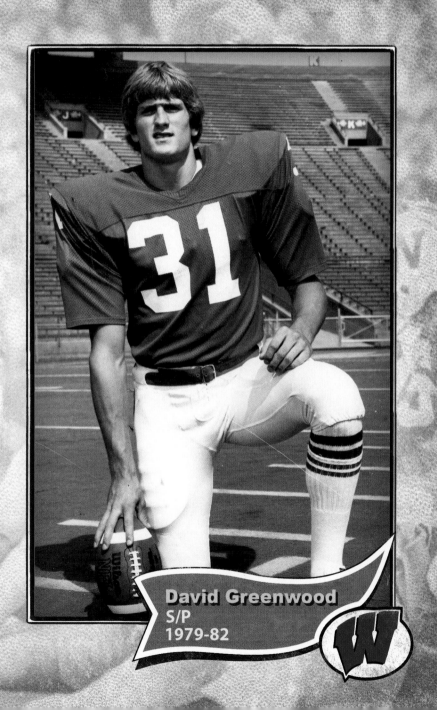

David Greenwood
S/P
1979-82

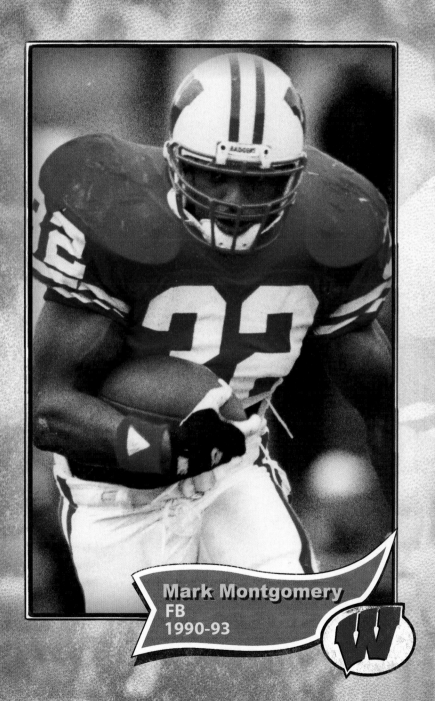

Mark Montgomery
FB
1990-93

The 1993 UW team that won Big Ten and Rose Bowl titles was led by an offense that gained more than 3,000 yards on the ground and converted at an amazing 58-percent clip on third down. Montgomery, a member of Barry Alvarez's first recruiting class, played a huge role in that offensive production by clearing the way for tailbacks Brent Moss and Terrell Fletcher. Montgomery started 34 games during his career and was selected in the seventh round of the 1994 NFL Draft by the Philadelphia Eagles.

33

When Dayne arrived at UW, one of his classmates, lineman Bill Ferrario, took one look at Dayne and figured he'd be competing with him for playing time. At 5-foot-10, 260 pounds, Dayne had the power of a lineman. He also had the grace and speed of a tailback. He used both to rack up a staggering 7,125 yards and 71 rushing TDs during his career at UW. As a senior, Dayne became the program's second Heisman Trophy winner and broke the NCAA record for career rushing yards with 6,397 (excluding bowl games). Dayne helped lead the Badgers to two Big Ten titles and was a two-time Rose Bowl MVP after combining for 446 yards in victories over UCLA and Stanford in Pasadena. Dayne's jersey was officially retired during the 2007 season.

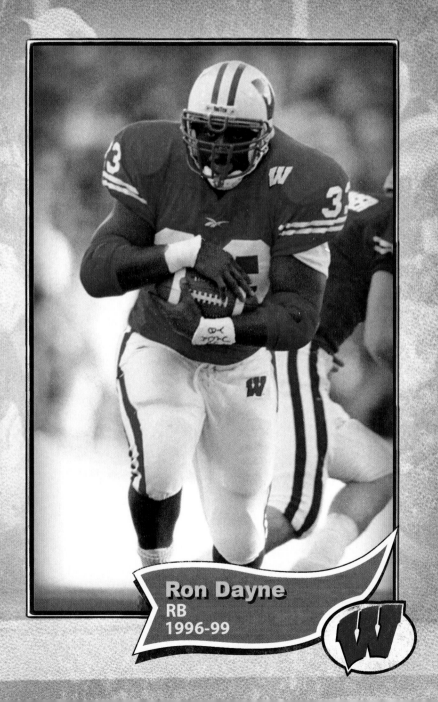

Ron Dayne
RB
1996-99

★ ★

★ ★ ★ ★ ★ ★ **TEN** ★ ★ ★ ★ ★ ★ ★

The Badgers didn't don numbers until the mid- to late 1920s, when the practice became widely adopted across all sports. There are 10 notables in UW football history in the era that predated numbers, starting with Pat O'Dea — a.k.a. The Kangaroo Kicker — who played from 1896-99 and is a member of the College Football Hall of Fame. For the full list, see page 124.

★ ★

34

Pat Harder | Back/Linebacker/Kicker | 1941-42 | Milwaukee, Wisconsin

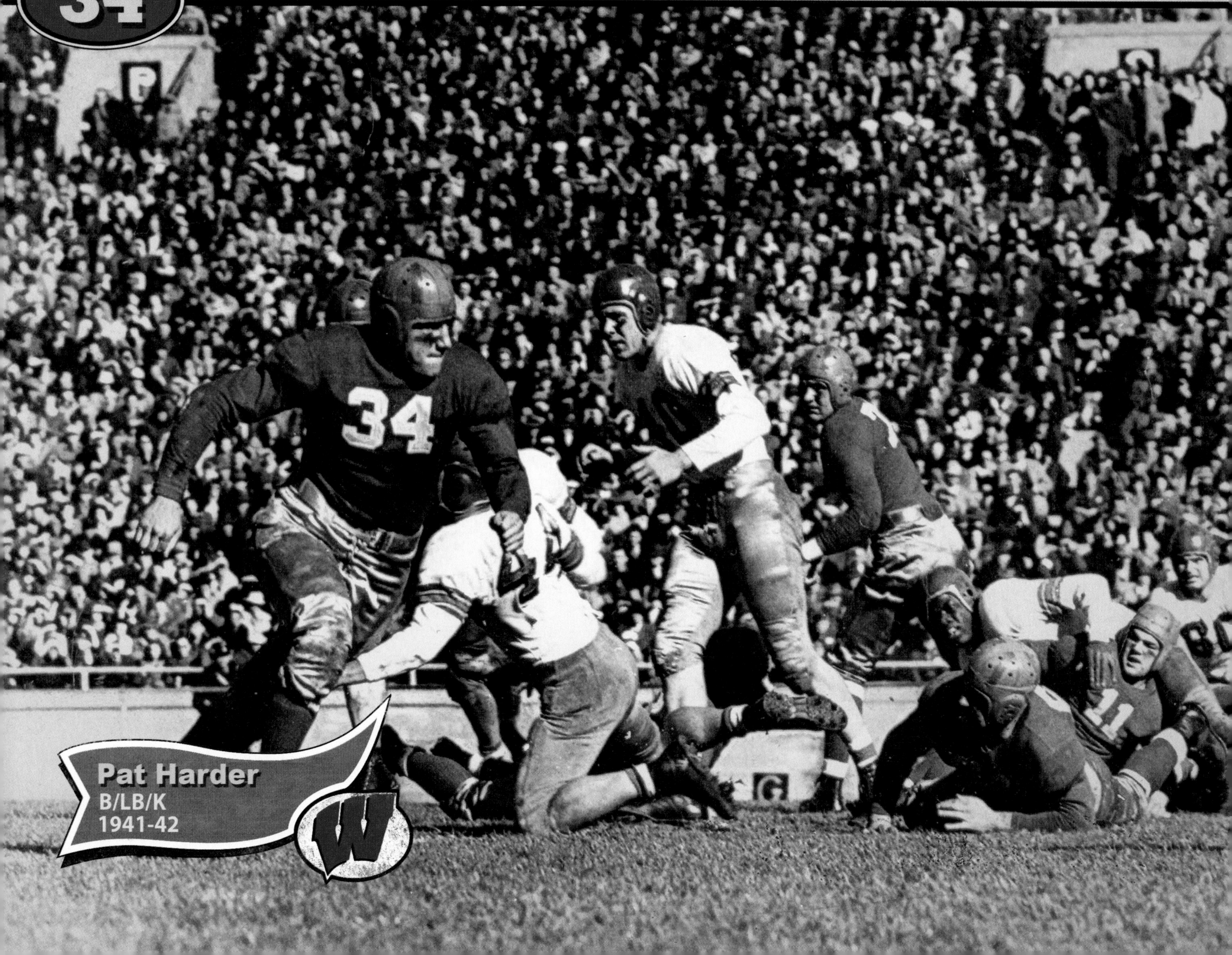

Pat Harder
B/LB/K
1941-42

One of the classic photos in the University of Wisconsin archives is from a 1942 football game between the Badgers and Ohio State.

A record crowd of 45,000 filled Camp Randall Stadium that day to watch sixth-ranked UW host the top-ranked Buckeyes.

As if the game needed any more buzz, it was Homecoming. It was also Halloween.

In the photo, Elroy "Crazylegs" Hirsch is carrying the ball on a sweep around the right side of the line of scrimmage as thousands of eyes in Sections P and Q on Camp Randall's northeast side are glued to his every move.

In front of Hirsch is Pat Harder. The fullback's pants are filthy and he has eye-black smeared across his face, which is also plastered with a look of determination while on a collision course with Ohio State linebacker and captain George Lynn, who is at the far right of the picture.

A better photo might have been what happened next, but we'll have to use our imagination. There's a pretty good chance Lynn ended up on his rear end after being hit by Harder, who earned the nickname "The Mule" during his time at UW. Fans would also chant "Hit 'em again Harder, Harder, Harder."

"When Harder arrived on the Madison campus, he brought a competitive fire that rubbed off on all his teammates," legendary *Wisconsin State Journal* sports reporter Tom Butler wrote in 1992 after Harder died at the age of 70 following a long illness. "He was a rough, tough character who lived for football."

The Badgers ended up beating the Buckeyes 17-7, with Harder scoring 11 points on a touchdown, field goal and two extra points.

A season earlier, Harder led the Big Ten Conference in rushing yards and scoring. He was an All-American in 1942 despite missing time with an ankle injury.

"His teammates talked about his ability to just ignore pain," said author Terry Frei, whose terrific book, *Third Down and a War to Go,* chronicled the 1942 Badgers, most of whom left school after the season to fight in World War II. "They just knew how tough it was for him."

Frei, whose father, Jerry, was an offensive guard for the Badgers and later a World War II pilot, had a major regret after finishing his book: that he didn't start the project sooner. By the time he started interviewing people for the book, many of the 1942 Badgers had died.

One of the Badgers Frei never got the opportunity to speak with was the fun-loving Harder, who drove around campus in a Model A. One scene Frei described in his book was Harder arriving late at practice one day and handing his speeding ticket to UW coach Harry Stuhldreher.

"I would have loved to swap stories with him," Frei said.

After serving in the Marines, Harder embarked on a successful NFL career. No UW player has been selected higher than Harder, the second overall pick in the 1944 NFL Draft. He played eight seasons in the NFL, leading the league in scoring three consecutive seasons.

One of those seasons was 1947, when Harder helped lead the then-Chicago Cardinals to an NFL title. Later, he was traded to Detroit and helped the Lions win back-to-back titles in 1952 and '53. Harder retired following the 1953 season and served as an NFL official for 17 seasons.

The Badgers rode "The Horse" a long way during his four seasons at UW. The Badgers went 26-8-3 during that span, including a Big Ten title in 1952. A three-time All-American, Ameche became the program's first Heisman Trophy winner in 1954 and ended his career as the NCAA's rushing leader with 3,345 yards. Ameche, who later was enshrined in the College Football Hall of Fame, was the third overall pick of the Baltimore Colts in the 1955 NFL Draft. He scored the winning touchdown in the Colts' 23-17 overtime victory over the Giants in the 1958 NFL title game, which was dubbed "The Greatest Game Ever Played." UW retired Ameche's No. 35 jersey.

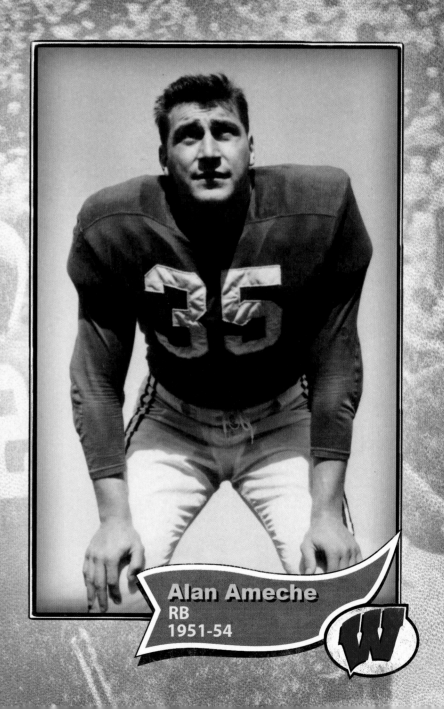

Alan Ameche
RB
1951-54

Girard had many titles besides his nickname, "Jug." He played quarterback, halfback and safety for the Badgers. He also punted and returned punts. Girard was an All-American for the Badgers in 1944 – at the age of 17. After a two-year hiatus for military service, Girard was convinced to return to school in 1947, when he set Big Ten and NCAA records with two punt return touchdowns in a game against Iowa. A first-round draft choice of the Green Bay Packers in 1948, he played 10 seasons professionally.

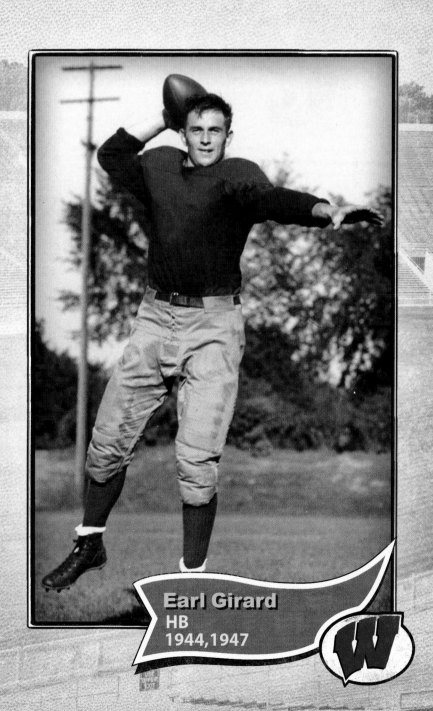

Earl Girard
HB
1944,1947

A four-year starter, Martin served as the lead blocker for NCAA all-time rushing leader Ron Dayne from 1996-98. He was the captain of the 1998 team that won Big Ten championship and Rose Bowl. Martin accomplished quite a bit off the field as well. He was named to the American Football Coaches Association inaugural "Good Works" team for community service and was cited for establishing an offseason program with UW Children's Hospital for players to visit hospitalized kids. Selected by the Philadelphia Eagles in the sixth round of the 1999 NFL Draft, Martin played five pro seasons.

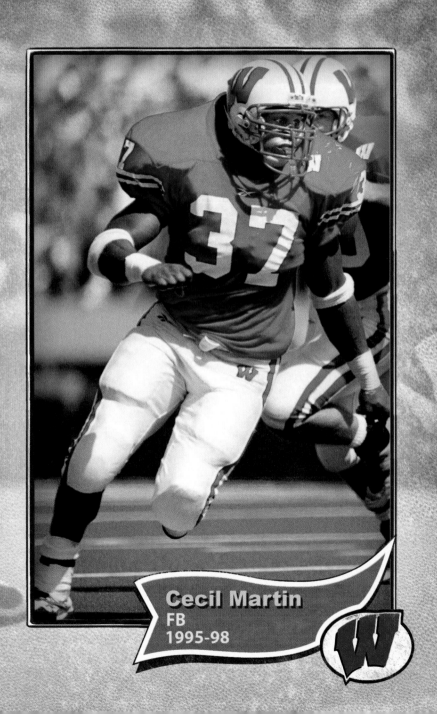

Cecil Martin
FB
1995-98

Odomes was a first-team All-Big Ten selection in 1986, when he had seven interceptions. He blocked two kicks in a game against Indiana in 1985. He was selected in the second round of the 1987 NFL Draft by Buffalo and lasted almost a decade in the league before the effects of a knee injury ended his career. Seven of those seasons came with the Bills, who reached the Super Bowl in four consecutive seasons during that span with the help of Odomes, a two-time Pro Bowl selection.

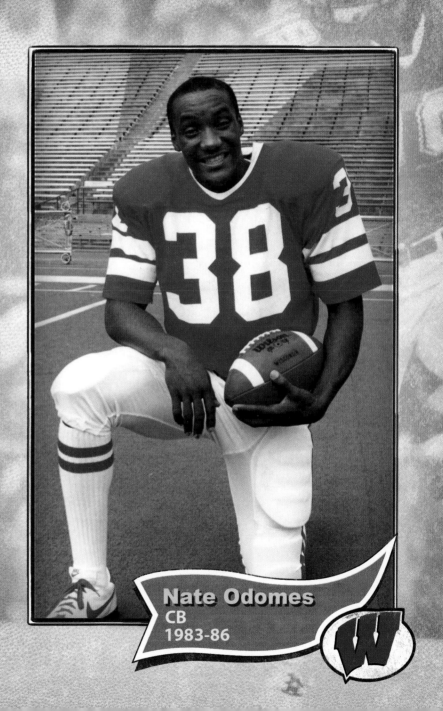

Nate Odomes
CB
1983-86

Long before Jimmy Leonhard, another walk-on safety from the state of Wisconsin developed into an All-American at UW. A two-time All-Big Ten selection, VandenBoom was the league's co-leader in interceptions as a junior in 1981 with six. Three of those came in a 21-14 victory over No. 1 Michigan in the season opener. VandenBoom was an All-American as a senior in 1982. He capped his career with an interception in UW's 14-3 victory over Kansas State in the 1982 Independence Bowl, the program's first-ever bowl victory. He was selected in the fifth round of the 1983 NFL Draft by the Buffalo Bills.

Matt VandenBoom
S
1980-82

"Crazylegs" played just one season for the Badgers, but what a fantastic one it was. He had 786 rushing yards, 390 receiving yards and 226 passing yards as UW went 8-1-1 in 1942. He played the next season at Michigan after enlisting in the Marine Corps and reporting to basic training in Ann Arbor. Hirsch went on to a Hall of Fame career in the NFL, finishing with 387 receptions for 7,029 yards and 60 touchdowns during a nine-year run with the Los Angeles Rams. Hirsch eventually returned to UW in 1969 – as the school's athletic director – and served 18 years in that capacity. Even after he retired, Hirsch was one of UW's greatest ambassadors. His No. 40 jersey is retired.

Elroy Hirsch
B
1942

After missing the 1929 season with a broken leg, Lubratovich returned the next season and earned consensus All-American honors for a UW team that went 6-2-1 and allowed just 20 points on the season. Lubratovich was selected to play in the East-West Shrine game following the season and went on to play five seasons with the NFL's Brooklyn Dodgers.

Milo Lubratovich
T
1928-30

★ ★

★ ★ ★ FORTY-SEVEN ★ ★ ★

Nearly half of our selections have played since Barry Alvarez stepped foot on campus as coach in 1990. Players whose careers bridged decades were placed into the decade in which they exhausted their eligibility.

2000s — 20	1970s — 11	1940s — 9
1990s — 27	1960s — 4	1930s — 4
1980s — 13	1950s — 9	1920s — 2

★ ★

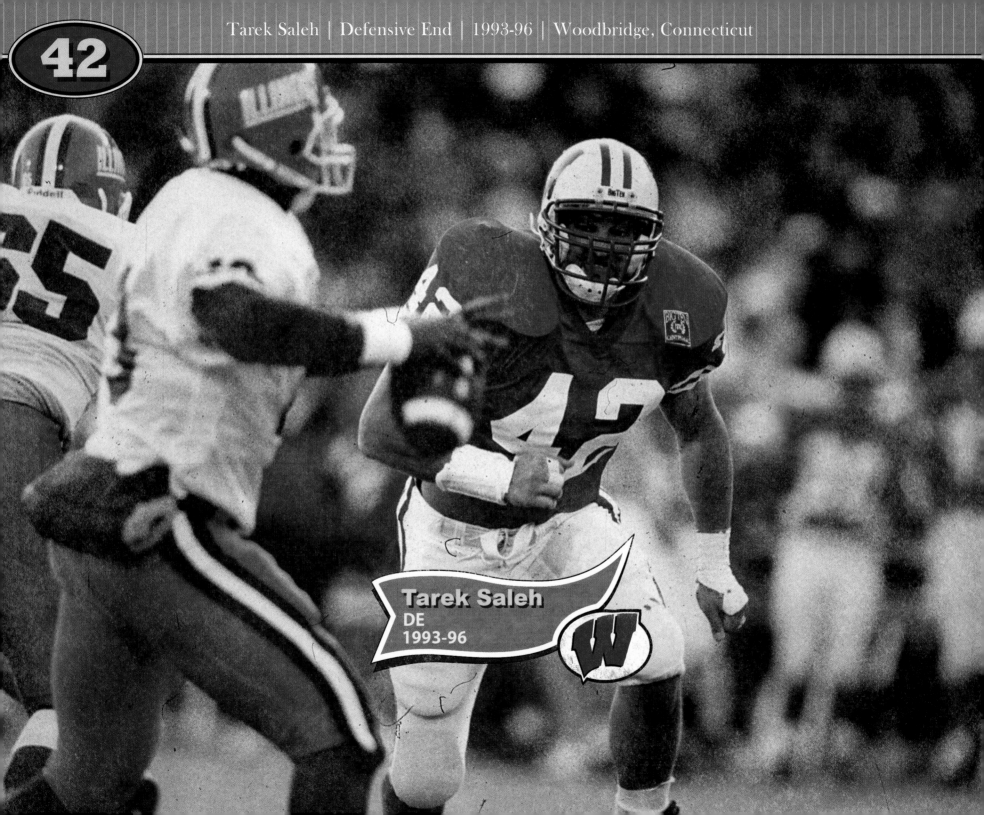

Tarek Saleh
DE
1993-96

Well over a decade removed from his last sack as a member of the Wisconsin Badgers, Tarek Saleh still feels very much a part of the program.

So much so that former coach Barry Alvarez likes to give Saleh a hard time about it.

"He thinks I signed him to a lifetime scholarship," Alvarez said. "I've told him that scholarship ran out after five years. It's not a lifetime deal."

Saleh can't help it. He loves to drop in at practice and will talk UW football any chance he gets.

That's what makes Friday nights during the football season so special to Saleh, who teams up with close friend and former UW teammate Derek Engler for a two-hour radio show on Madison's ESPN affiliate, WTLX-FM/100.5, called "In the Trenches."

The show is equal parts informative – Saleh and Engler, who both played in the NFL, know their football – and hilarious because of the chemistry between the two buddies.

"Derek's one of my best friends and we enjoy talking football," Saleh said. "We have a lot of fun."

It's easy to talk about UW football when the program is winning. Saleh admits it's somewhat a challenge to critique the Badgers when they struggle.

"I definitely want to be respectful," he said. "But to be respectful, I don't think you have to sugarcoat things too much. Being respectful is understanding that No. 1, the players are student-athletes, they're not paid professionals.

"I was in the sport. I'm not so easy, like the rest of the world, to go and kick someone in the groin. But we call a spade a spade, tell it like it is. But we do it without kicking their dog."

Saleh knows better than to take himself too seriously during the radio gig.

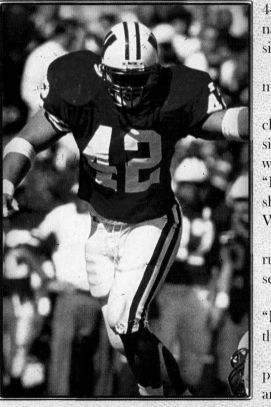

"I don't see it as necessarily being a career," he said, "but it's something to kind of keep involved with sports."

So is his regular job as a national sales manager for Impact Sports, an apparel printing/embroidery company based in the Madison area.

Sales is a perfect fit for the affable Saleh.

"I'm definitely a people person," he said.

That Saleh and his family – he's married with 4-year-old twin daughters – have settled in Waunakee, a Madison suburb, is notable when you consider he was raised in Connecticut.

In fact, Saleh never would have come to UW if his mother had her way.

"His mother, you've got to explain to your bridge club where your son's going, and it's more impressive to say Penn State because they identify more with Penn State than with Wisconsin," Alvarez said. "I think he showed a lot of individualism and really showed strength by making the decision to come to Wisconsin."

Saleh made his mark at UW as a relentless pass-rusher, earning first-team All-American honors as a senior in 1996.

"He didn't know how to slow down," Alvarez said. "He played one speed; that's the way he played all the time."

Saleh was a bridge between two eras at UW. He played in the 1994 Rose Bowl as a true freshman, and was a senior when Ron Dayne burst onto the scene as a freshman.

Thirteen years later, he still holds the school record for career sacks (33) and tackles for loss (58), which generates mixed emotions.

"I'm very proud of that," Saleh said. "I'm happy to still have those records, but I'd definitely like to see the Badgers have more sacks. I'd probably lose the record, but that's not such a bad thing."

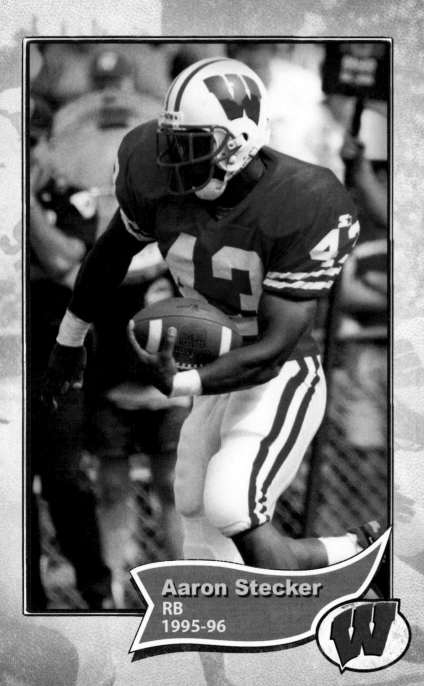

Aaron Stecker
RB
1995-96

Stecker is one of four UW players with a 100-yard kickoff return. That return, at Minnesota, was the longest in the nation in 1995; Stecker also rushed for 114 yards in that victory over the Gophers. Stecker had a punt return for a touchdown as a sophomore in 1996, but decided to transfer to Western Illinois following that season after it became apparent that future Heisman Trophy winner Ron Dayne would be getting most of the carries. Stecker completed his ninth NFL season in 2008; he was a member of the Tampa Bay Buccaneers team that won the Super Bowl in 2003.

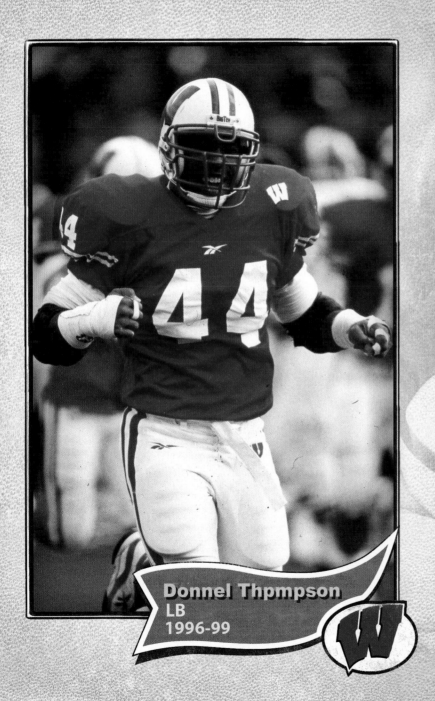

Donnel Thpmpson
LB
1996-99

One of the great walk-on stories at UW – a broken arm in his senior season at Madison West scared off recruiters -- Thompson was a team captain of the 1998 and '99 teams that won Big Ten and Rose Bowl titles. He's 10th in career tackles at UW with 347 and is one of only four two-time winners of the Jay Seiler Coaches Appreciation award. Thompson made the Pittsburgh Steelers' roster as an undrafted free agent in 2000 and played three seasons in the NFL, finishing with the Indianapolis Colts.

45

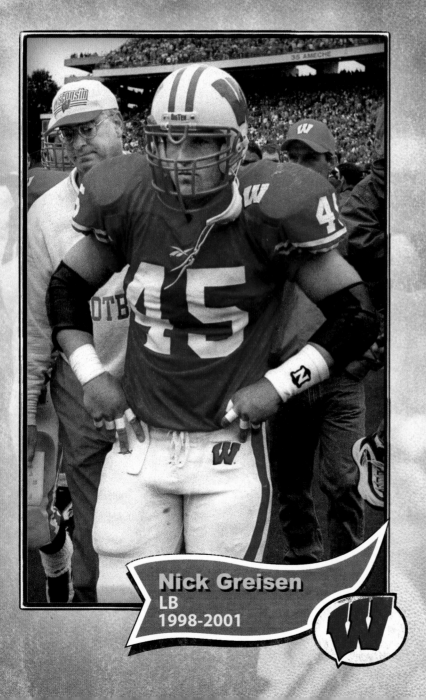

Nick Greisen
LB
1998-2001

Greisen's older brother Chris made it to the NFL as a quarterback. Nick Greisen liked to think of himself as the quarterback of UW's defense. A dependable middle linebacker, he was a two-time first-team All-Big Ten selection. His 337 tackles are 13th all-time at UW. Greisen was selected by the New York Giants in the fifth round of the 2002 NFL Draft and completed his seventh NFL season in 2008.

Jeff Mack
LB
2000-03

A second-generation Badger – his father, Jeff Sr., was a star receiver at UW from 1972-74 – Mack was hampered by neck and back injuries that curtailed his sophomore and junior seasons but still started 38 games during his career. As a senior, he was a team captain and shared the team lead in tackles with 98. Mack, who graduated from Madison West High School, sold soft drinks at Camp Randall during UW football games while he was growing up.

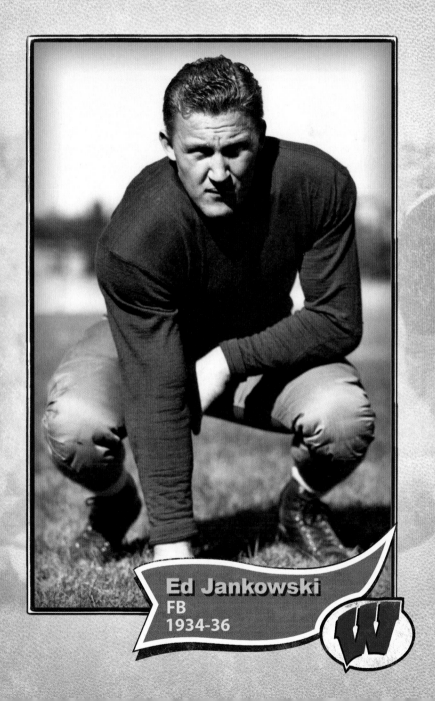

Ed Jankowski
FB
1934-36

A two-time team MVP, Jankowski was a first-round draft pick of the Green Bay Packers in 1937. He played five seasons with the team, was selected to the Pro Bowl during the NFL championship season of 1939 and was elected to the Packers' Hall of Fame. During his senior year at UW, Jankowski blocked for Howie Weiss, who two years later became one of just seven Badgers to claim Big Ten Player of the Year honors. Regarded by newspaper accounts of the time as a "vicious" tackler who "takes savage delight in bodily contact," Jankowski, according to an advance scout from Minnesota, "punishes himself without stint, but he breaks the other fellow in two when he hits him. He takes a terrific battering but murders the opposing line and on defense he often meets the ball carrier at the scrimmage line and drives him back several yards."

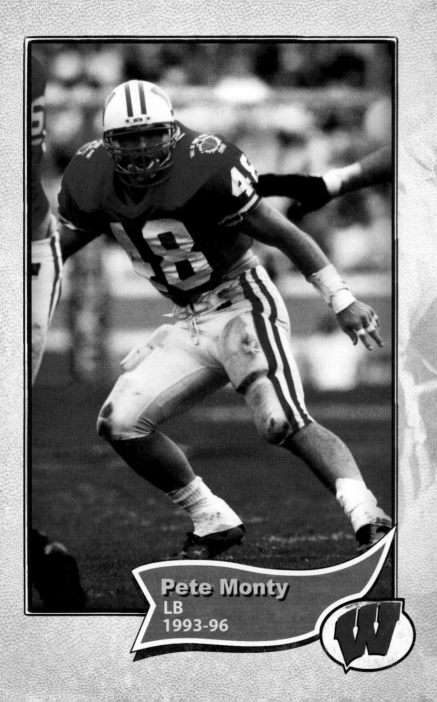

Pete Monty
LB
1993-96

Monty is the program's career leader in tackles with 451. He led the Badgers in tackles three consecutive seasons and was named first-team All-Big Ten and team MVP as a senior in 1996. A true warrior, the 6-foot-2, 249-pound Monty made 35 consecutive starts, a streak that included coming back from a torn knee ligament to play after a bye week. A two-time captain, Monty had a younger brother, Joe, who also played for Wisconsin. He was selected by the New York Giants in the fourth round of the 1997 NFL Draft and played four pro seasons.

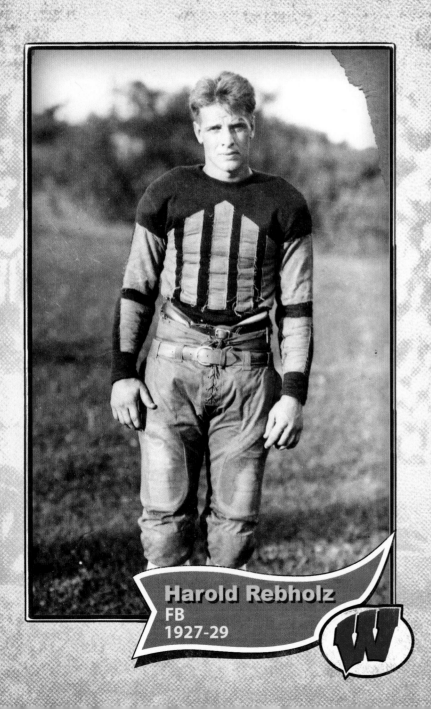

Harold Rebholz
FB
1927-29

Rebholz rushed for over 900 yards during his career despite being one of the lightest fullbacks in the Big Ten at 166 pounds – this at a time when one of his key blockers, Milo Lubratovich (No. 41 on this list), was considered a "giant" at 225 pounds. As a senior in 1929, Rebholz – also regarded as one of the best defensive backs in the Big Ten – was the Badgers' MVP and was named an honorable mention All-American. The following summer he accepted a commission to West Point. He also played hockey at UW.

★ ★

★ ★ ★ ★ NINETEEN ★ ★ ★ ★

Players from 19 states made our list. Predictably, Wisconsin has produced the majority of selections, with 54, followed by Illinois (16), Minnesota (5), Missouri and New Jersey (3), and Florida, Michigan, Ohio and Pennsylvania (2). Ten states had one player each: Colorado, Connecticut, Georgia, Indiana, Iowa, New York, North Carolina, North Dakota, Texas and Virginia.

★ ★

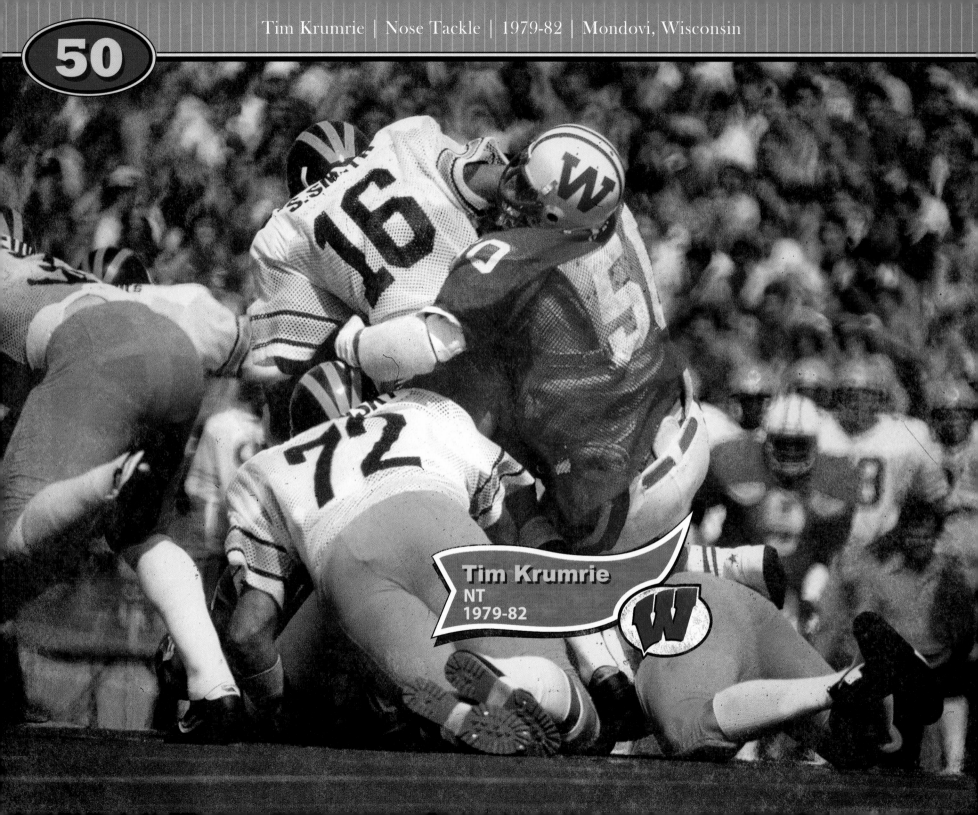

Tim Krumrie
NT
1979-82

Tim Krumrie had experienced some rough times during his long career in the National Football League.

But nothing quite compared to the 2008 season, his 26th in the NFL as either a player or assistant coach.

The Kansas City Chiefs finished with a 2-14 record, better only than the winless Detroit Lions.

The Chiefs had many fatal flaws, one of which was an anemic pass rush. Minus All-Pro defensive end Jared Allen, who was traded to the Minnesota Vikings during the offseason, the Chiefs produced just 10 sacks; by comparison, the Dallas Cowboys led the NFL with 59 sacks.

Changes were inevitable, and coach Herm Edwards and his staff were fired in late January.

That left Krumrie, a defensive line coach in the NFL since his playing career ended following the 1994 season, in professional limbo. That he had been in this position before – Krumrie was an assistant in Cincinnati and Buffalo before coming to Kansas City – helped make the uncertainty more tolerable.

"There's not a manual for coaching when you get hired and fired," Krumrie said. "You've got to go through it a few times and feel it and understand what's happening.

"The worst thing you can do is lose confidence in yourself and your ability. If you think you're a good coach, you (had) better stick to your guns and go down swinging."

Which is exactly what Krumrie did. Less than a month later, Krumrie had a job ... as the defensive line coach for the Kansas City Chiefs. He was the only defensive assistant on Edwards' staff who was rehired by new coach Todd Haley.

"Tim is about football," Haley told Bob Gretz, who has covered the Chiefs for nearly three decades and now maintains his own website, bobgretz.com. "You've got to pull the reins on him every once in a while, but I think he's as passionate as they come. He's tough as nuts in every area. He's what we want our players to be – mentally tough guys that cannot be affected by anything."

Mental toughness is something Krumrie requires of his players. He's known around the league for a grueling workout he conducts with NFL prospects prior to the draft.

"It's more of a character check and a heart check," Krumrie said of the routine, in which he engages in hand-to-hand combat with the players. "Numbers are numbers. A lot of guys can run great and look good in their underwear. But when they really have to compete with somebody one-on-one, much like a wrestler going on a wrestling mat, it's you and the other guy, and when these kids come in front of me it's me and them.

"I haven't missed on too many players doing that. I can pretty much peg 'em."

The tenacious Krumrie, who started all 46 games during his UW career, was a three-time, first-team All-Big Ten pick and two-time, first-team All-American for the Badgers at nose guard despite being undersized and not very athletic. He still holds the school record for solo tackles (276) and has the most career tackles among defensive linemen with 444.

An afterthought as a 10th-round draft pick of the Cincinnati Bengals in 1983, Krumrie developed into an All-Pro performer who helped the Bengals reach Super Bowl XXIII. He left that game, a 20-16 loss to the San Francisco 49ers, with a gruesome injury – he broke his leg while attempting to tackle Roger Craig – but was back in time for the 1989 season opener less than eight months later.

"Growing up, my hero for the Badgers was Tim Krumrie," said former UW standout Don Davey, who was voted the Badgers' best all-time player to wear No. 99. "Here's a guy that wasn't very talented physically – he was kind of short and not very fast – but he made every tackle up and down the line of scrimmage. That was kind of who I molded myself after."

Krumrie coaches the same way he played, and he has no intention of changing his ways anytime soon.

"This is my life," Krumrie said. "This is really all I know and it's all I want to do. I guess I was one of the fortunate ones to make it this long."

51

Webster was a first-team All-Big Ten pick and the Badgers' MVP in 1973. Nicknamed "Iron Mike," he was a nine-time Pro Bowl selection during a Hall of Fame NFL career that spanned 17 seasons. Webster, a key member of the Pittsburgh Steelers organization that won four Super Bowls in the 1970s, was named to the NFL's 75th anniversary team.

Mike Webster
C
1971-73

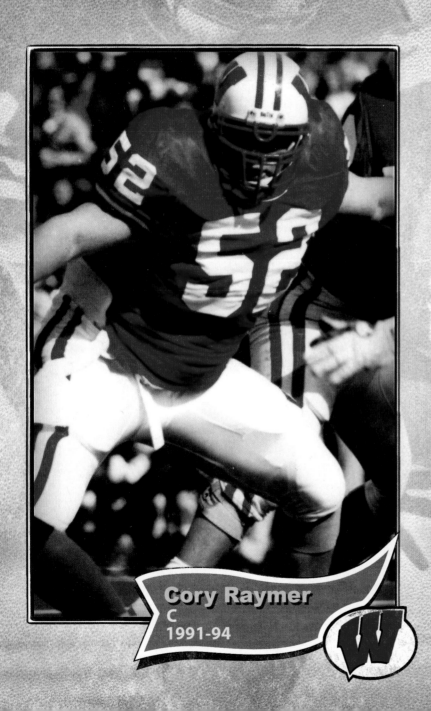

Cory Raymer
C
1991-94

Another in a long line of great centers at UW, Raymer was two-time, first-team All-Big Ten pick and a consensus All-American in 1994. As a junior, he played on an offensive line that helped the Badgers average 250 rushing yards per game en route to a Big Ten championship and Rose Bowl victory. Raymer was selected in the second round of the 1995 NFL Draft by the Washington Redskins and played 11 seasons professionally.

A three-time team MVP, Wilson was the Big Ten's MVP and a third-team AP All-American in 1949. He was named to Wisconsin's all-time team during a voting by fans in conjunction with the centennial celebration of college football in 1969. Wilson, nicknamed "Red," was also a star baseball player at UW. He was picked in the fourth round of the 1950 NFL Draft but opted to play baseball instead. He played 10 seasons professionally for the Chicago White Sox, Cleveland Indians and Detroit Tigers.

Robert Wilson
C
1946-49

54

Messner was first-team All-Big Ten and captain of the 1954 team that went 7-2, earning honorable mention All-America honors in the process. A center for as long as he played organized football – dating to his enrollment at Madison East High School in 1948 -- Messner, who was just 20 years old as a senior, helped clear space that season for Alan Ameche, who became the program's first Heisman Trophy winner.

Gary Messner
C
1952-54

55

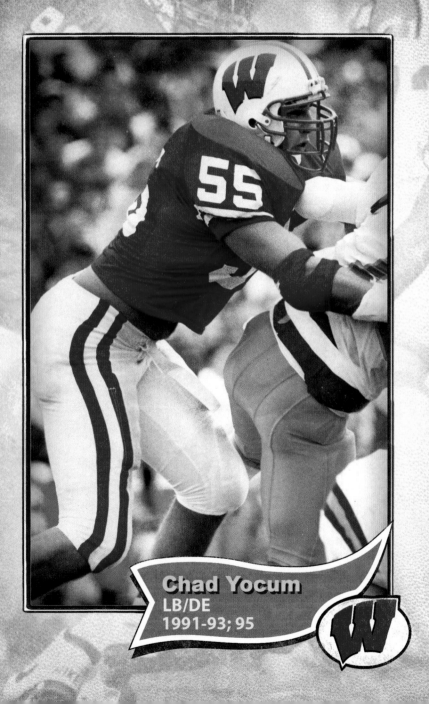

Chad Yocum
LB/DE
1991-93; 95

Yocum made an immediate impact at UW. As a true freshman, he tied for second in the Big Ten with two fumble recoveries. As a sophomore, he was named honorable mention All-Big Ten and had three sacks in UW's upset victory over No. 12 Ohio State. But a back injury derailed his career. He missed all but three games during the 1993 and '94 seasons, then returned as a fifth-year senior and started six games in 1995.

Frank Molinaro
C
1930-32

Atwo-way player who earned the nickname "60-Minute Moon" during his career. Molinaro was a second-team All-Big Ten pick at tackle in 1932, when the Badgers went 6-1-1. He also played on the 1930 team that went 6-2-1. Molinaro was president of the National "W" Club in 1961-62 and president of the Mendota Gridiron Club in 1963-64.

57

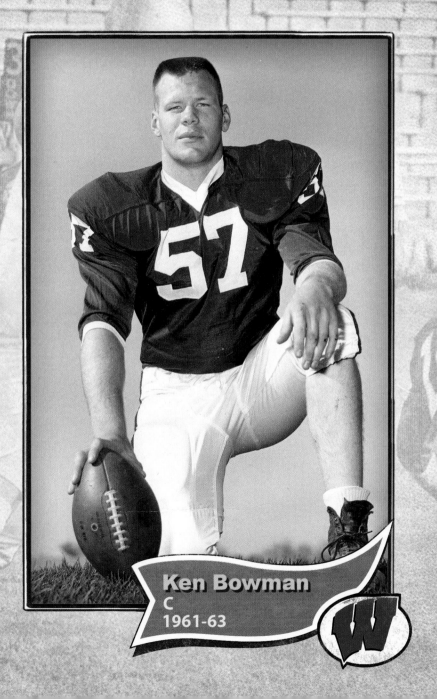

Ken Bowman
C
1961-63

A team captain and first-team Academic All-American in 1963, Bowman was also a member of the 1962 team that won a Big Ten title and advanced to the Rose Bowl. He was named to Wisconsin's all-time team during a voting by fans in conjunction with the centennial celebration of college football in 1969. Bowman played 10 seasons in the NFL with the Green Bay Packers. He played on two Super Bowl title teams and was the center on Bart Starr's famous quarterback sneak in the Ice Bowl.

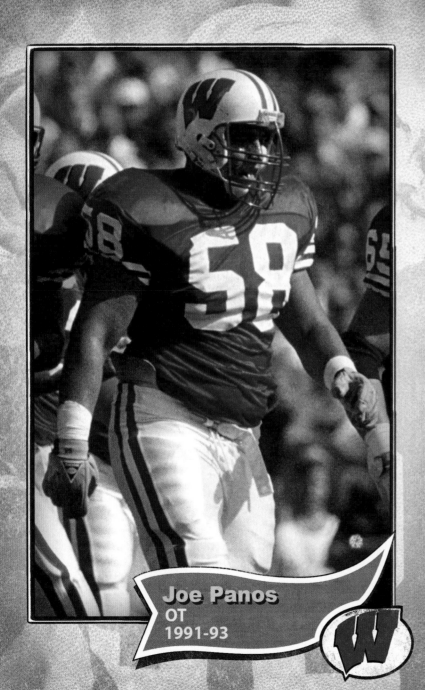

Joe Panos
OT
1991-93

Regarded as one of the great leaders in program history, Panos opened eyes early in the 1993 season when, asked about UW's chances of winning a Big Ten title, he posed, "Why not Wisconsin?" The Badgers did win the Big Ten – and the Rose Bowl – with the help of Panos, a first-team All-Big Ten pick and second-team All-American. Panos was selected by Philadelphia Eagles in third round of 1994 NFL Draft and played seven pro seasons, finishing with the Buffalo Bills in 2000.

Mario Pacetti
OL
1932-34

P acetti was a star athlete and honor student at UW. Not only did Pacetti play guard for the Badgers, he also served as the team's place-kicker. His 50-yard field goal gave UW its only points during a 6-3 loss to Minnesota in the 1933 finale. A story in the *Wisconsin State Journal* about Pacetti's death said the "young giant ... played with such skill and fire that he had won the name of 'Wisconsin's Iron Man.'" Unfortunately, that obituary came far too soon. Pacetti, who had been accepted to the U.S. Military academy in West Point, committed suicide in June 1935, about seven months after he had finished his UW career.

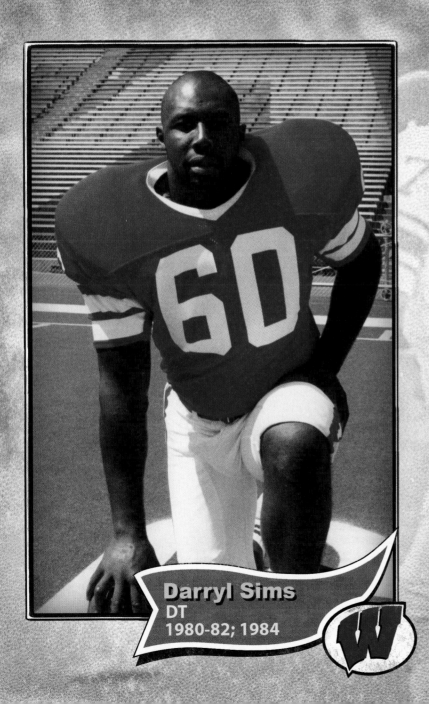

Darryl Sims
DT
1980-82; 1984

A three-time first-team All-Big Ten selection, Sims led the Big Ten in tackles for loss as a junior with 22. He had four sacks – including a safety – during a victory over Northwestern in 1982. He was selected by the Pittsburgh Steelers in the first round in 1985 – joining teammates Al Toon and Richard Johnson as first-round picks – and played four seasons in the NFL.

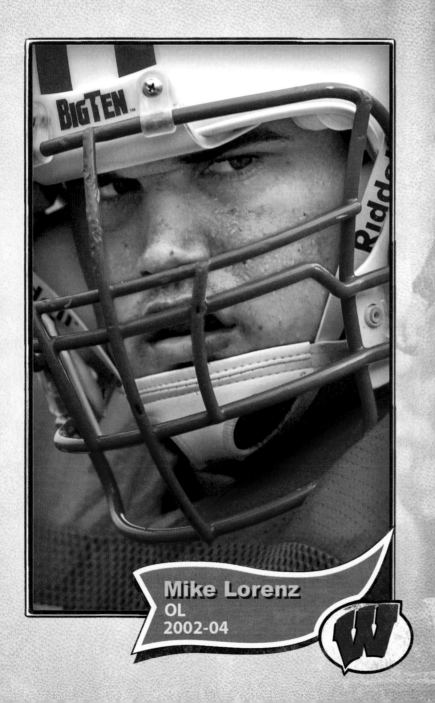

Mike Lorenz
OL
2002-04

Barry Alvarez called Lorenz one of the biggest overachievers he ever coached. Lorenz started every game as a junior and was a part-time starter as a senior. He served as an inspiration off the field by earning Academic All-Big Ten honors despite being diagnosed with dyslexia as a child.

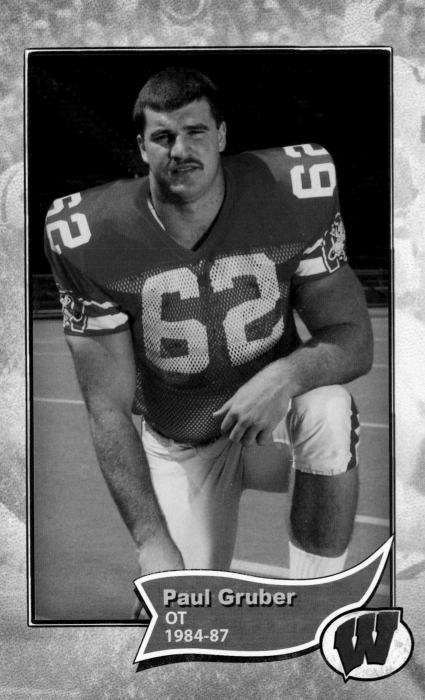

Paul Gruber
OT
1984-87

The Badgers only won three games when Gruber was a senior captain in 1987, yet he earned first-team All-Big Ten honors and was named an All-American. Gruber was taken fourth overall by the Tampa Bay Buccaneers in the 1988 NFL Draft and became a trailblazer when he held out until signing a five-year contract worth $3.8 million, making him the highest-paid offensive lineman in the NFL. Up until that point, only skill players earned that kind of money. Gruber played 12 seasons with the Buccaneers, earning three Pro Bowl nods along the way.

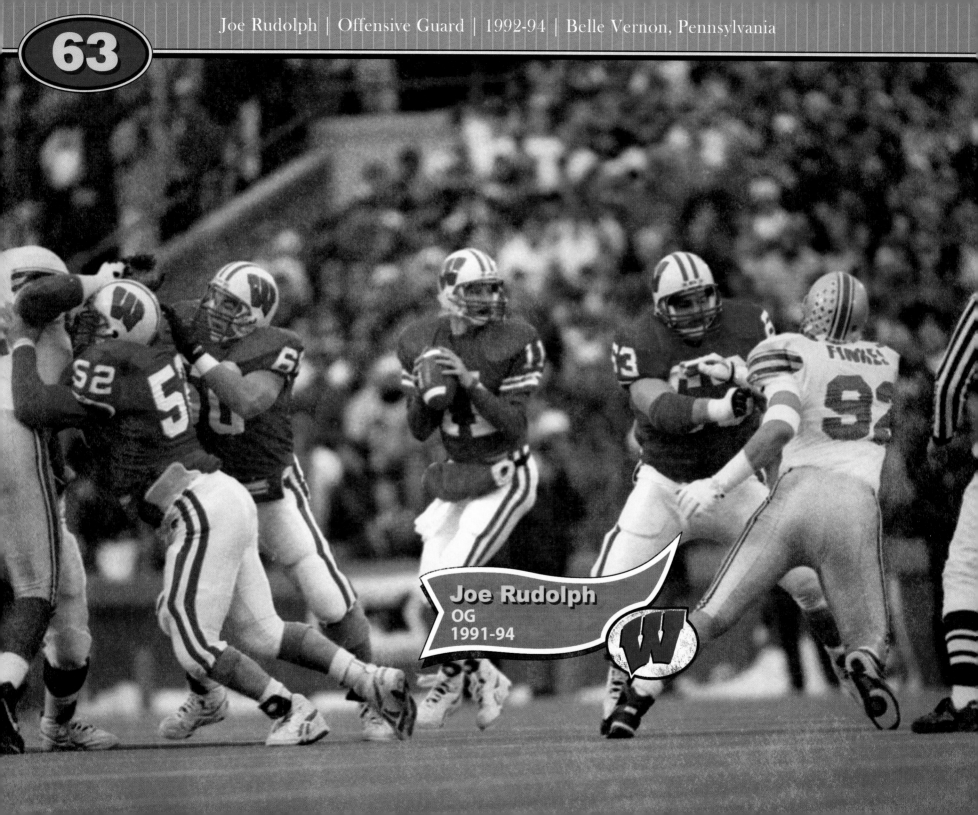

Joe Rudolph
OG
1991-94

Joe Rudolph doesn't have to search for the right words when he sits in recruits' living rooms.

It's a simple case of speaking from the heart for the University of Wisconsin assistant coach.

"I feel comfortable going in and selling Wisconsin because it's what I experienced," said Rudolph, a two-time first-team All-Big Ten left guard for the Badgers. "It's what I know. It's what I believe in."

Rudolph made that statement shortly after being hired as UW's tight ends coach in February 2008. Since then, you could make a strong case that he's been the Badgers' most valuable recruiter.

Speaking from the heart has its advantages, admits Rudolph, who makes it clear from his first contact with recruits that he's a proud UW alum.

"As a recruit, the amount of information that you're receiving and trying to absorb is a lot to handle," he said. "When you can speak in specifics and put it in a sense that is a little more real to them, you hope some of that sticks.

"I want them to know that when I speak to them about the community and the university and the reputation that carries with you and the diploma you take away and the respect that you get being part of this program, I'm speaking from experience."

Rudolph produced some impressive results on and off the field during his first season back at UW. He helped the Badgers land four prospects from the state of Ohio – a state that has been very good to UW over the years – in the 2009 recruiting class. Included in that group was highly touted defensive end Pat Muldoon.

Tight end also continued to be a position of strength for the Badgers despite the loss of senior Travis Beckum, who sustained a season-ending

knee injury midway through the season. Garrett Graham took over the featured role from Beckum and earned first-team All-Big Ten honors after leading the Badgers in receiving.

Meanwhile, little things like receiving his players' academic reports from classes Rudolph took at UW have prompted flashbacks to his playing days.

"It's a lot of fun to be back here working for a program that you feel so strongly about," Rudolph said.

Rudolph took an interesting path back to UW. After a brief NFL career, he set out for a career in business and even earned a master's degree in business administration from the prestigious Tepper School of Business at Carnegie Mellon University in Pittsburgh.

But Rudolph's mind kept drifting back to football, even during class projects, so he followed his passion.

He spent three seasons at Ohio State – two as a graduate assistant, one as a strength coordinator – and another at Nebraska before being hired by UW coach Bret Bielema.

It's been almost 20 years since Rudolph arrived at UW as a member of Barry Alvarez's first recruiting class. That group served as the foundation for the 1993 team that won a Big Ten Conference title, beat UCLA in the Rose Bowl and, more importantly, put Wisconsin football back on the map.

"We came in with a belief that Wisconsin can be special and that was provided through coach Alvarez and the staff," Rudolph said. "They really delivered that message and had us believing it. In believing that message, we believed in them. Everybody wanted to find a way to contribute. They really wanted to find a way to be the best they could be."

Ken Currier
OL
1942; 1946-47

Currier started at right guard for the 1942 team that went 8-1-1. He returned for the 1946 and '47 seasons after serving as a flight instructor in World War II. According to Terry Frei's book, *Third Down and a War to Go*, Currier turned down a contract offer from the Green Bay Packers in 1948 because he preferred more stable and long-term employment.

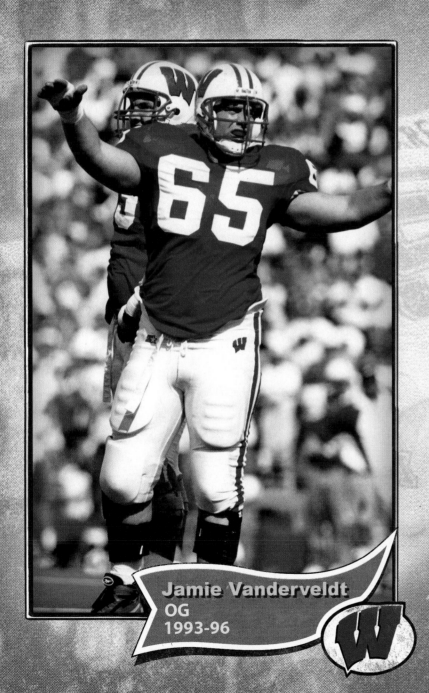

Jamie Vanderveldt
OG
1993-96

Vanderveldt arrived on campus as an All-American defensive lineman out of Waukesha Catholic Memorial but promptly was switched to offense. After seeing substantial time as a reserve in each of his first two seasons, VanderVeldt earned first-team All-Big Ten honors at left guard in 1996, the same season freshman Ron Dayne set a UW single-season mark with 2,109 rushing yards. He started 30 games in his career and was named captain as a senior.

Thompson was a key piece of Barry Alvarez's rebuilding project at UW. He was a starter on the 1993 team that won a Big Ten title and beat UCLA in the Rose Bowl, then was a captain and a first-team All-Big Ten selection as a senior. Thompson is second at UW in career tackles for loss (57) and third in sacks (28). He's 16th all-time in tackles with 316. Thompson was selected by the Cincinnati Bengals in fourth round of the 1995 NFL Draft and played six pro seasons.

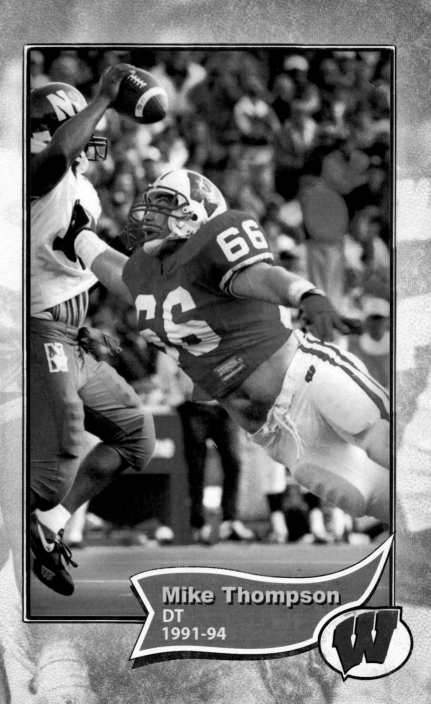

Mike Thompson
DT
1991-94

Dan Buenning
OG
2001-04

Buenning was a fixture in UW's lineup for four seasons. He started 49 games, including the final 36 of his career. As a senior, Buenning was a first-team All-Big Ten selection and was named a first-team All-American by *College & Pro Football Newsweekly*. He also was captain that season for a team that won its first nine games and rose to No. 5 in the national rankings. Buenning was selected by the Tampa Bay Buccaneers in the fourth round of the 2005 NFL Draft and completed his fourth professional season in 2008.

Just a few weeks before the start of the 1975 season, Stieve wondered if his days of playing football were over. He was struggling with stiff legs, the result of offseason knee surgery. Stieve's career wasn't finished – far from it. Part of a group referred to as "Marek's Marauders," Stieve was a first-team All-Big Ten pick and team captain that season while helping pave the way for Billy Marek. Stieve played nine seasons in the NFL with the New Orleans Saints and St. Louis Cardinals.

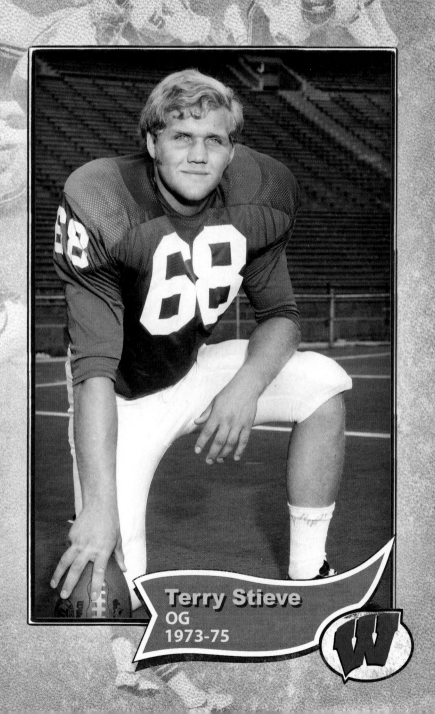

Terry Stieve
OG
1973-75

Engler was a key reserve whose versatility allowed him to regularly find time in the lineup before taking over the starting job at center as a senior. He helped pave the way for true freshman Ron Dayne, whose 2,109 rushing yards still stand as a single-season record at UW. Engler spent four seasons in the NFL and played on the New York Giants team that advanced to the 2001 Super Bowl.

Derek Engler
C
1994-96

A big reason Billy Marek left UW in 1974 as the school's all-time leading rusher was the blocking of Lick, his high school teammate at Chicago St. Rita. A two-time first-team All-Big Ten pick, Lick was a consensus All-American in 1975. He was drafted eighth overall by the Chicago Bears in 1976 and played six seasons in the NFL.

Dennis Lick
OT
1972-75

71

Suminski was an All-American in 1952, when the Badgers were ranked No. 1 in the nation for the first and only time in program history, won the Big Ten title and advanced to the first bowl game in school history, the Rose Bowl. Suminski helped clear the way that season for standout running back Alan Ameche, who became the first player in school history to top the 1,000-yard mark. Suminski played for the Washington Redskins in 1953 and became an All-Pro in the Canadian Football League while playing for the Hamilton Tiger Cats from 1957-59.

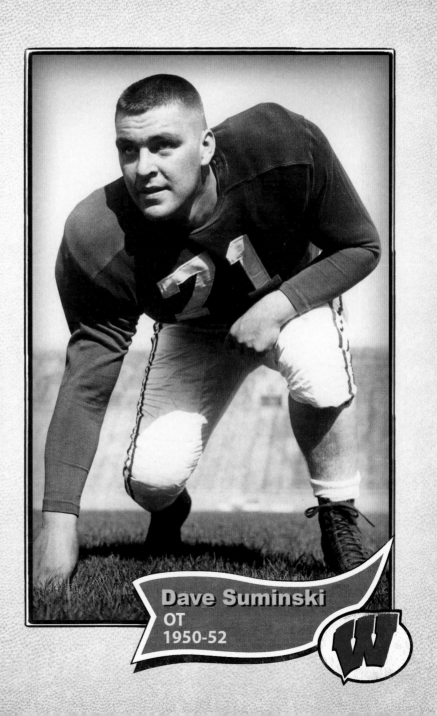

Dave Suminski
OT
1950-52

72

Thomas already had accomplished a lot – he was an All-American and first-team All-Big Ten pick in 2005 – when he decided to return for his senior season at UW following a serious knee injury in the Capital One Bowl. It turned out to be an excellent decision. Thomas returned to the field for the start of next season and went on to earn All-American honors and win the Outland Trophy. He also was a captain and co-MVP of a team that won a school-record 12 games. Thomas, who was named a National Scholar-Athlete by the National Football Foundation, was selected by the Cleveland Browns with the third overall pick in the 2007 NFL Draft and earned a trip to the Pro Bowl as a rookie.

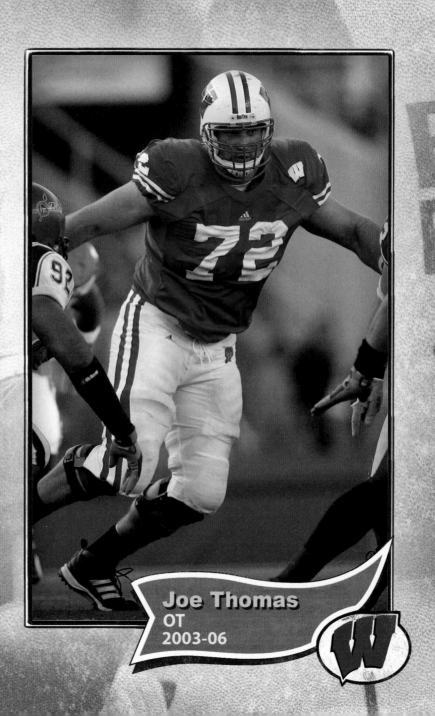

Joe Thomas
OT
2003-06

A second-generation Badger – his father, George, was a star lineman at UW in the 1930s – Lanphear was an All-American and first-team All-Big Ten selection as a senior as the Badgers advanced to their second Rose Bowl. Lanphear was named to Wisconsin's all-time team during a voting by fans in conjunction with the centennial celebration of college football in 1969. He played two seasons in the NFL with the Houston Oilers.

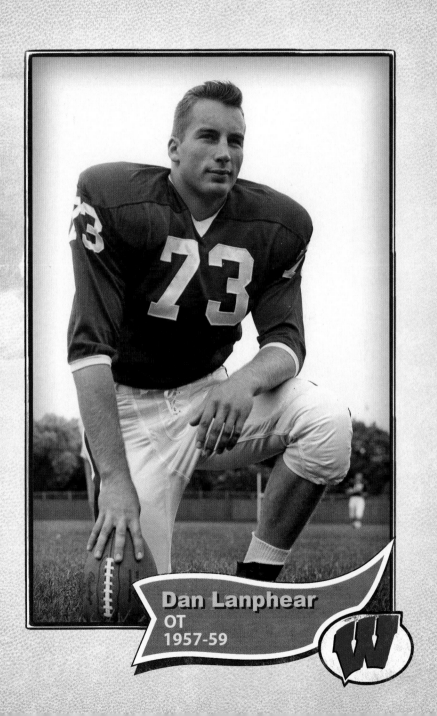

Dan Lanphear
OT
1957-59

74

Burke had arguably the greatest season by a defensive player in program history in 1998 when he led the nation with 22 sacks and 31 tackles for loss – both program records – en route to being named the Big Ten's Defensive Player of the Year. A season earlier, he was named UW's MVP. Burke, who is second at UW in career sacks (32) and third in tackles for loss (54), played four seasons in the NFL with the Arizona Cardinals.

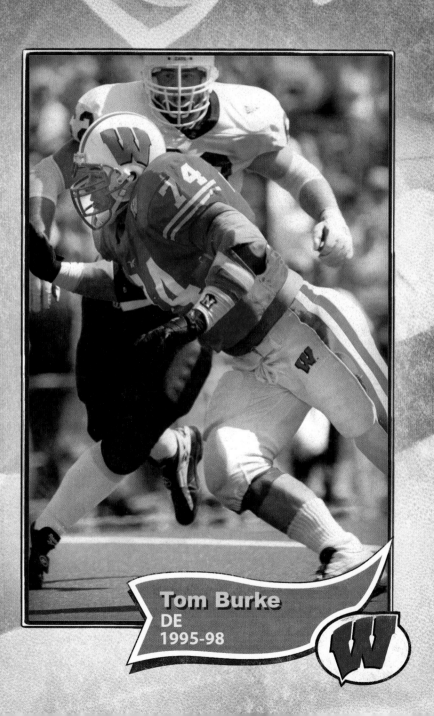

Tom Burke
DE
1995-98

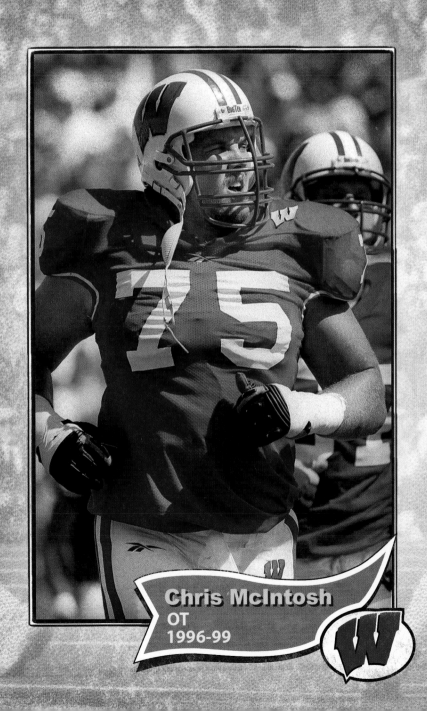

Chris McIntosh
OT
1996-99

With New Year's Eve just a few days away and the Badgers in California preparing for the 2000 Rose Bowl, Barry Alvarez was asked who he'd want with him in the event of any Y2K issues. "I'd take Big Mac by my side," he said. Alvarez knew he could count on McIntosh, a captain on the 1998 and '99 Big Ten and Rose Bowl title teams. As a senior, McIntosh was a consensus All-American and finalist for the Outland Trophy. He was drafted in the first round of the 2000 NFL Draft by the Seattle Seahawks but was limited to just two seasons as a pro due to a neck injury.

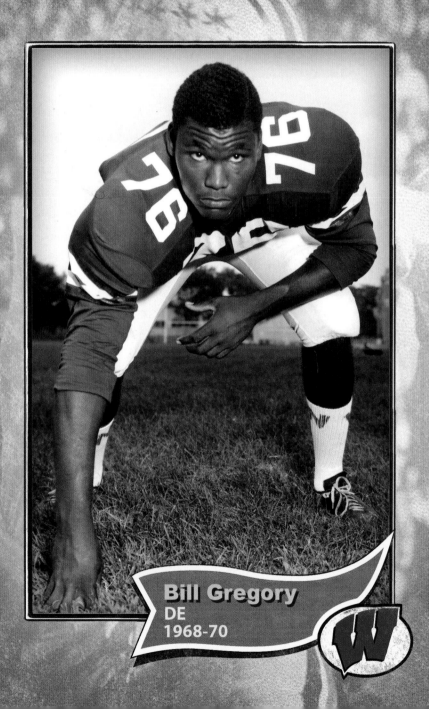

Bill Gregory
DE
1968-70

Gregory spoke like a leader before UW hosted No. 16 Penn State on Oct. 3, 1970. "When we play each other, they're just another team," Gregory said of the Nittany Lions. "They've got the same number of players on the field at the same time and they put their pants on the same way we do." Gregory, a two-time team captain, was right. The Badgers won the game 29-16, its first victory over a ranked opponent in eight years. UW finished with four victories that season – its most since 1963 – with the help of Gregory, a first-team All-Big Ten selection. He was selected in the third round of the 1971 NFL Draft by the Dallas Cowboys and played in four Super Bowls during his 10 seasons in the league.

★ ★

★ ★ ★ ★ ★ **EIGHT** ★ ★ ★ ★ ★

Eight Badgers have been inducted into the College Football Hall of Fame, including five players honored in this book: Dave Schreiner, Pat Harder, Elroy Hirsch, Alan Ameche and Pat Richter. The others are Pat O'Dea, Robert Butler and Marty Below. George Little (1925-26) is in as a coach.

★ ★

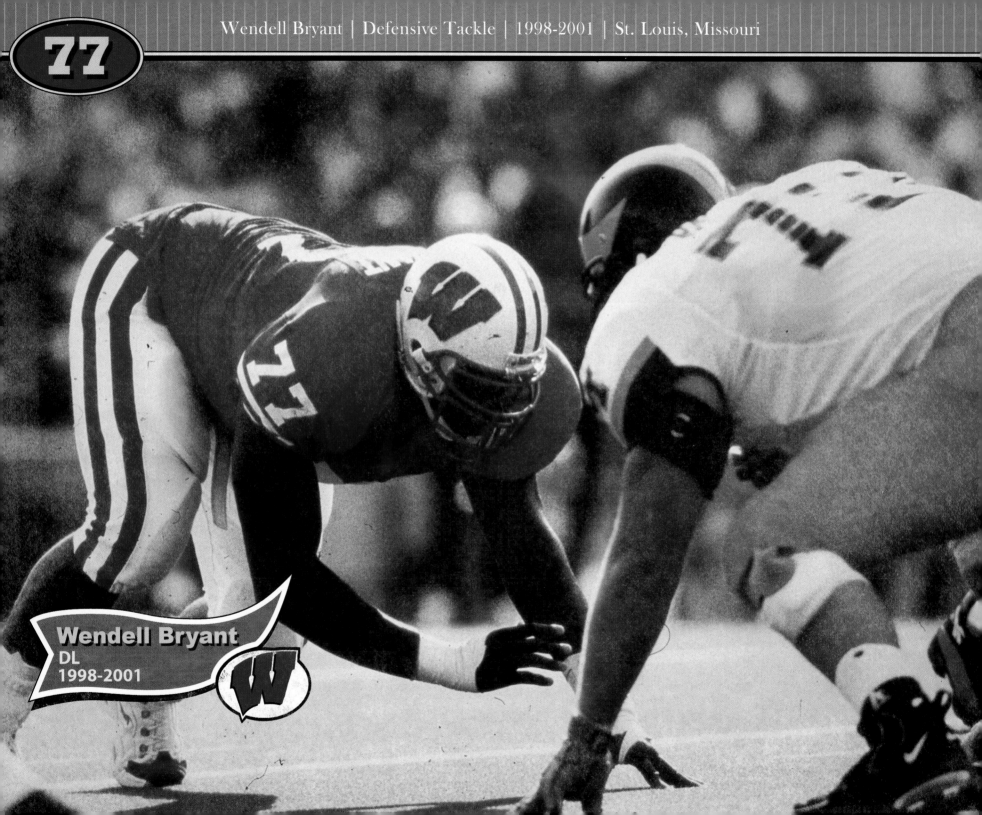

Wendell Bryant
DL
1998-2001

Wendell Bryant had seen family members' lives wrecked by drug and alcohol abuse.

It couldn't happen to him, Bryant told himself, even as he spent mornings stoned and evenings drunk.

Those people were losers. He, on the other hand, was an NFL player, a former first-round pick.

"I had this attitude of arrogance about the whole thing," Bryant said. "It got to the point where it took my career away from me and took significant money away from me and kind of brought me back down to zero."

Suddenly, it dawned on Bryant.

"I was a loser," he said.

Bryant doesn't mind talking about it, because it's part of the rehabilitation process. Bryant says he's been clean and sober since June 2008, when he finally decided to end the spiral of destruction that had cost him his career.

For many, Bryant's fall from grace was sad to watch. At UW, where he was a three-time first-team All-Big Ten selection and earned All-American honors as a senior, Bryant was a favorite of fans and media types because he was smart, funny and honest.

He was a good football player and a good person. "He was a model citizen with us," former Badgers coach Barry Alvarez said.

But Bryant changed when he got to the NFL. By 2005, he had been kicked out of the league after breaking the league's substance abuse-policy for the third time.

In three seasons with the Arizona Cardinals, he started just nine games. The 12th overall selection in the 2002 draft was a bust of epic proportions.

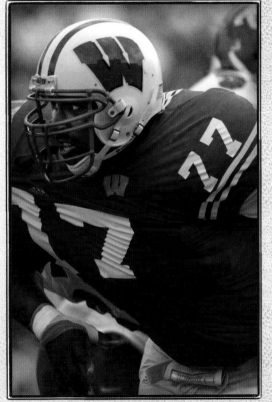

Alcohol and marijuana were the main culprits, although Bryant admits he also dabbled in Ecstasy.

He had hit rock bottom but began his climb back with the help of two emotional events in his life. The first was the birth of his daughter, Devyn, in November 2007. The second was the death of his grandfather, Norman Wells, two months later.

Bryant entered rehab in the summer of 2008 and began to get his life back in order. He finally got around to earning his degree from UW – he finished two classes online – and decided he wanted to play football again.

He knows it won't be easy. Factors working against Bryant are his age (he'll turn 29 in September 2009) and the fact he's been out of football for almost five years.

And then there's the tag that Bryant, who has vowed to return part of the $5.5 million signing bonus he received from Arizona, will carry around with him for the rest of his life: substance abuser.

"Something like that follows you," Bryant said. "But I don't look at that as a negative thing. I look it as, I'm somebody I hope people can learn from."

Bryant doesn't know what his football future holds. He desperately wants to get back in the NFL and had tryouts in the offseason with the Buffalo Bills and Detroit Lions. He'll give the new United Football League a try in order to enhance his profile.

However, football is a secondary priority for Bryant.

"I have a choice in the matter now as to whether to stay clean or go back out there on that bad road," said Bryant, who's fifth all-time at UW with 24 sacks. "My worst day in recovery is better than my best day when I was out there using."

A four-year starter for the Badgers, he played a key role on defenses that ranked first (1998) and fifth (1999) nationally in points allowed per game. Both of those teams won Big Ten and Rose Bowl titles. Kolodziej was also a standout on the UW track and field team. He was 230th overall selection in the 2001 NFL Draft – the New York Giants took him in the seventh round – but lasted seven seasons as a pro.

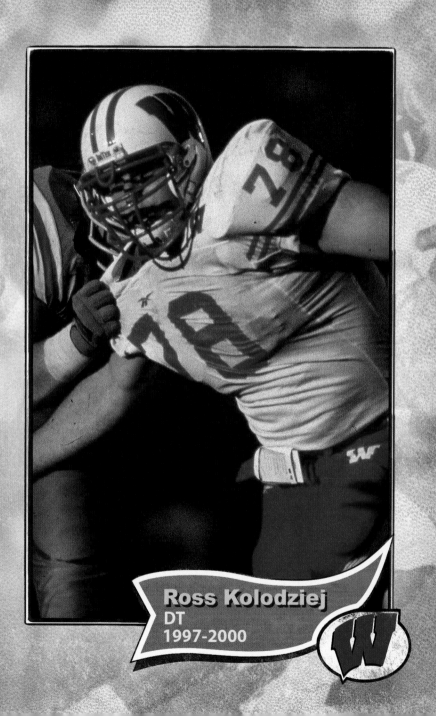

Ross Kolodziej
DT
1997-2000

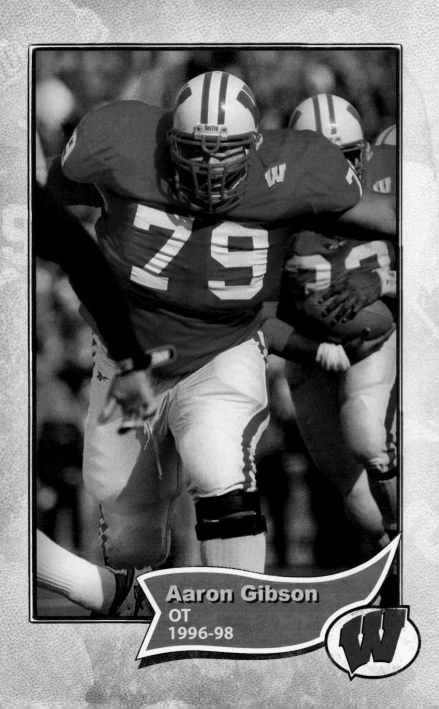

Aaron Gibson
OT
1996-98

Gibson arrived in Madison weighing over 400 pounds. He created a big legacy by the time he left. Gibson, whom Barry Alvarez called "the most dominant player I ever coached," was a consensus All-American and a finalist for both the Lombardi Award and Outland Trophy as a senior in 1998, when the Badgers won their first of back-to-back Big Ten and Rose Bowl titles. Gibson was a first-round pick in the 1999 NFL Draft – he was selected 27th overall by the Detroit Lions – and played seven seasons in the NFL.

Schreiner was a two-time All-American, including a consensus choice and the Big Ten MVP when the Badgers went 8-1-1 in 1942. The first UW player to have three TD receptions in one quarter, Schreiner averaged 20 yards per catch. Teams rarely tested his side on defense. That season was the last time Schreiner, who was selected by the Detroit Lions in the second round of the 1944 NFL Draft, would play organized football. Schreiner left UW to serve in World War II. He was a lieutenant in the Marines when he was killed in the Battle of Okinawa in 1945. A few months later, UW retired his number.

Dave Schreiner
E
1941-42

Faverty was an All-American and the team's MVP when the Badgers went 7-1-1 in 1951. He starred on the famed "Hard Rocks" unit that allowed the fewest points per game in the nation that season. Faverty, who also wore No. 85 at UW, was named United Press Lineman of the Week twice. He played professionally for the Green Bay Packers in 1952.

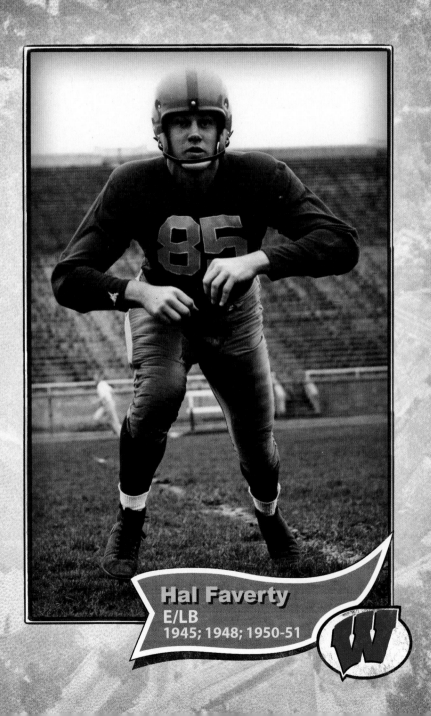

Hal Faverty
E/LB
1945; 1948; 1950-51

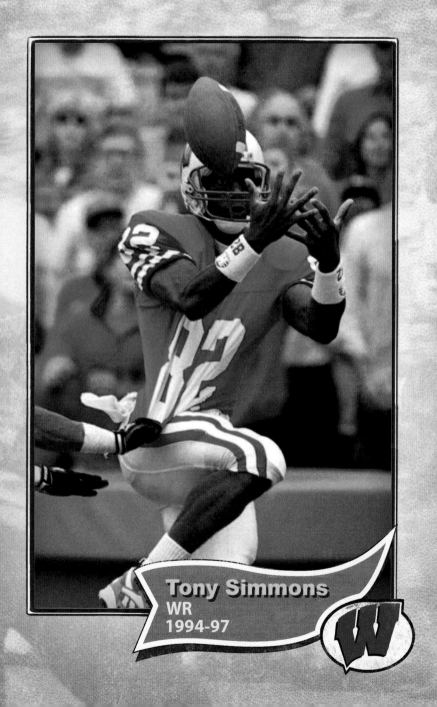

Tony Simmons
WR
1994-97

A big-play threat throughout his career, Simmons is the program's all-time leader in average yards per reception (20.1). He's second at UW in career touchdown receptions (23) – he earned the name "Touchdown Tony" during his time in Madison – and sixth in receiving yards (1,991). Simmons was selected in the second round of the 1998 NFL Draft by the New England Patriots and played five seasons in the pros.

Allan Shafer
QB
1944

Shafer was injured during a game against Iowa at Camp Randall Stadium on Nov. 11, 1944, and died later that day at a Madison hospital. An autopsy revealed that Shafer, a 17-year-old freshman from Madison West High School, had died of hemorrhage of the lungs, the result of a violent blow; he was helped off the field but collapsed on the sidelines and did not regain consciousness. It was the last time somebody wore No. 83 for the Badgers. Shafer's parents joined the team the following Saturday for a game at Michigan. The family also established a scholarship that is still awarded today in Shafer's name.

A hometown product out of Madison East High School, Hayes led the Badgers in receiving yards as a junior and senior. He finished his career 10th in both receptions (106) and receiving yards (1,575), no small feat at a time when the offense focused heavily on the running game, especially in his final two seasons with Ron Dayne in the backfield. Hayes played two games for the UW men's basketball team in the 1995-96 campaign before concentrating on football. He was drafted in the fourth round by the Carolina Panthers in 1998 and played five seasons in the NFL.

Donald Hayes
WR
1994-97

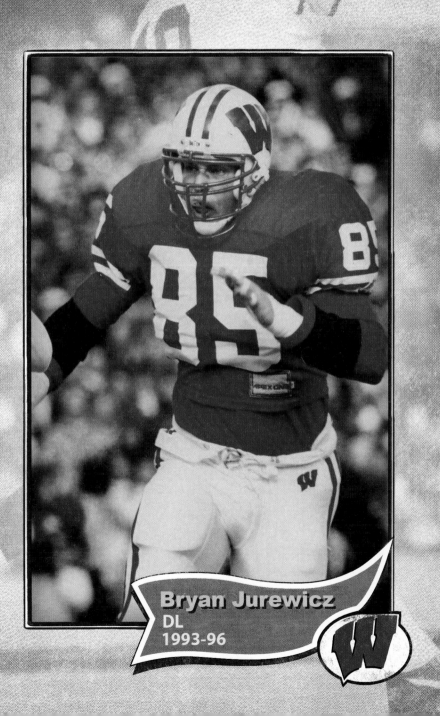

Jurewicz started 41 games during his career, including UW's victory over UCLA in the 1994 Rose Bowl, while rotating between outside linebacker, defensive end and defensive tackle. He recorded 26 career tackles for loss – including 15 as a senior -- and set a program record with nine passes defensed. Jurewicz was just as impressive off the field. As a senior in 1996, he was UW's Ivan Williamson Scholastic Award winner and a second-team Academic All-American.

Bryan Jurewicz
DL
1993-96

86

Ron Leafblad
E
1962-64

Leafblad was a starter on 1962 Big Ten championship team that lost a thriller to USC in the Rose Bowl. He caught a touchdown pass in a 14-9 victory over Minnesota to clinch that trip to Pasadena; the Badgers were ranked No. 3 in the nation at the time, while Minnesota was ranked fifth. A valuable two-way player noted for his blocking at tight end, Leafblad was a team captain as a senior in 1964.

★ ★

★ ★ ★ ★ **EIGHTEEN** ★ ★ ★ ★

Of the 18 Badgers to earn Academic All-American honors, 10 are featured in this book, including Don Davey, who earned the honor in each of his four seasons at UW (1987-90). The others are Alan Ameche (1953-54), Dale Hackbart (1959), Pat Richter (1962), Ken Bowman (1963), Matt VandenBoom (1982), Bryan Jurewicz (1996), Jim Leonhard (2003-04) and Joe Thomas (2006).

★ ★

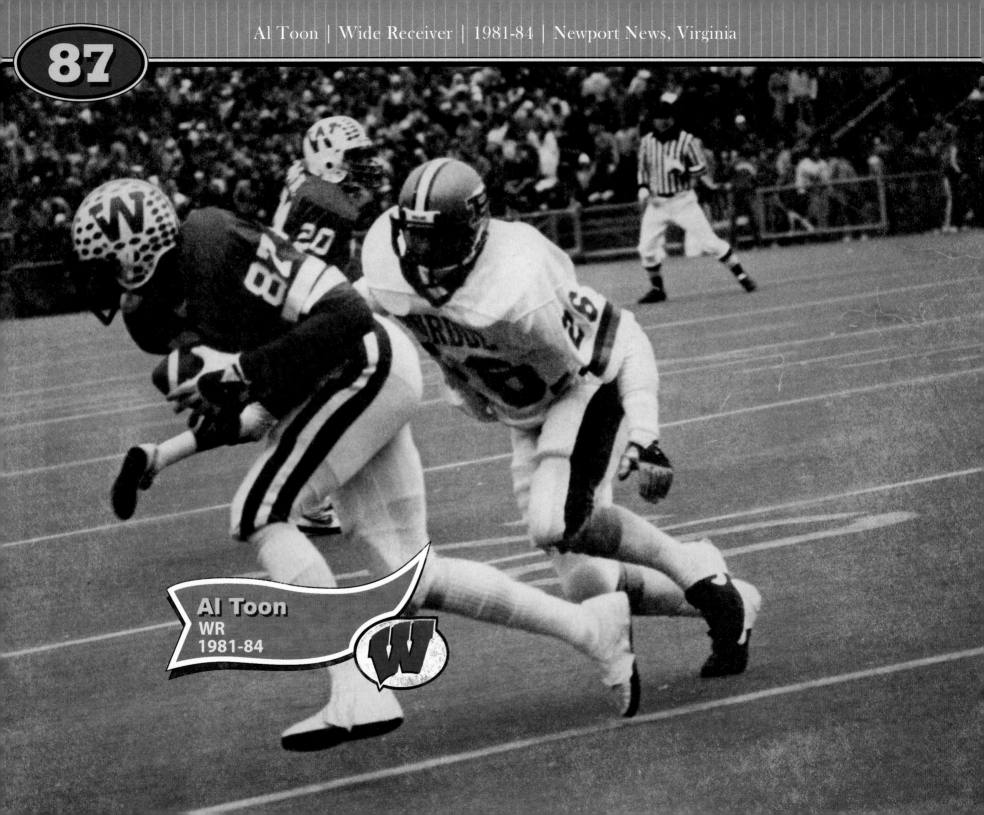

Al Toon
WR
1981-84

Al Toon can't sit still as it is. Now imagine him at one of his kids' sporting events, which elicit strong feelings that leave his stomach tingling with excitement one minute and genuine concern the next. There's the thrill of seeing his children compete at a high level, whether it's son Nick playing at the same venue – Camp Randall Stadium – where Toon created so many highlights as a record-breaking wide receiver back in the 1980s, or his three daughters on the volleyball court. Kirby is a preferred walk-on at UW, Molly is a senior at Middleton High School and is headed to Michigan on a full scholarship, and Sydney is a freshman at Middleton.

Then there's the agony of worrying about the welfare of those children.

The fear of injury is a concern for any parent. For Toon, it's at another level because of the pain he endured from playing the sport he loved. He doesn't want his children to feel that pain.

Yet Toon is realistic. He knows athletes get injured. Already, Nick has dealt with a nagging hamstring injury and Kirby missed part of her senior season in volleyball because of a torn anterior cruciate ligament in her knee.

"Those things are just part of playing at a high level of athletics," Toon said. "But this is the path that they've chosen."

It's the path their father chose, too. A native of Newport News, Va., Al left UW as the program's all-time leader in receptions (131), receiving yards (2,103) and touchdown receptions (19) – he's now fourth, third and fourth, respectively, on those lists – and was the 10th overall pick in the 1985 NFL draft.

By all accounts, Toon had a great NFL career. He had 517 receptions for 6,605 yards and 31 touchdowns and was elected to the Pro Bowl three times in eight seasons with the New York Jets.

But that career was cut short by concussions. The last – believed to be the ninth one Toon sustained during his career – came midway through the 1992 season during a game against the Denver Broncos.

What followed – the effects of post-concussion syndrome – was even worse. Toon, who had three young children at the time, spent six weeks in bed immediately following his retirement, according to a 1994 story in *Newsday*. Later side effects included dizziness – triggered by seeing moving objects, like ceiling fans – fatigue and irritability.

"There were some dark days," said Jane Toon, Al's wife and also a UW alum. "But he has come through doing just great and never complained. He always got done what needed to get done and he just kind of kept on, went about his business and went about the business of raising a family and getting back to normal after his retirement."

The good news is that Toon has felt good – really good, actually, he says – for the last decade. Life after football has moved at a quick pace because Toon keeps himself busy with an assortment of business investments.

In addition to finding his niche in commercial real estate, Toon also helped start Capitol Bank with eight others in 1995; another branch opened in 2007. He also serves on the board of directors for the Green Bay Packers and National Guardian Life, a mutual insurance company in the Madison area.

"He isn't somebody who sits around," Jane Toon said. "Even when we're home, he's always doing something: putzing in the yard, doing something in the house, doing something in the garage."

Saturdays are surreal for Jane Toon because she sees a lot of her husband in her son. Nick had 17 receptions for 257 yards and a touchdown as a redshirt freshman wide receiver for the Badgers in 2008.

Because of the risk of injury, Al never encouraged Nick to play football. But he never discouraged it, either.

"It's been quite exciting," Al said. "He's extremely dedicated to the sport. He just loves everything about it, which is what I would have hoped for if he chose to go in that direction. It's just kind of fun seeing him starting to excel."

88

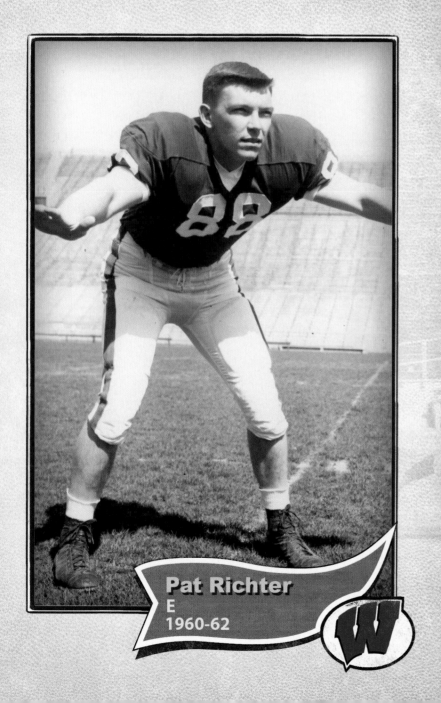

Pat Richter
E
1960-62

Richter was a big part of two golden eras in UW football. He was a consensus All-American, Academic All-American and team captain during the 1962 season, when the Badgers won the Big Ten title and advanced to the Rose Bowl. UW fell to USC in a 42-37 thriller that for decades was regarded as the best-ever game in Pasadena, but Richter, a former Madison East standout who also played basketball and baseball at UW, set Rose Bowl records with 11 receptions for 163 yards. Those records stood for 31 years, until J.J. Stokes of UCLA broke them against Wisconsin. Richter, who played eight seasons in the NFL with the Washington Redskins, became UW's athletic director in 1989. His best decision was hiring Barry Alvarez to resurrect a football program that won three Rose Bowls in a span of seven seasons. Richter's No. 88 jersey was retired by UW during the 2006 season, and he was immortalized with a bronze statue at the Kellner Hall entrance to Camp Randall.

Albert Hannah
WR
1969-71

Pat Richter, who was still with the Washington Redskins, liked what he saw of Hannah during a visit to a UW football practice in 1970. "He has the potential to be one of the best," Richter told the *Wisconsin State Journal*. The running and end-zone celebrations of Rufus Ferguson stole the spotlight in those days, but Hannah did distinguish himself as a big-play threat. He averaged 17.4 yards per reception during his career, which ties him for sixth at UW. As a senior in 1971, he led the Badgers with 608 receiving yards on 39 receptions.

It was quite a year for Voss in 1952: Not only was he an All-American for a UW football team that won a Big Ten title and earned the program's first Rose Bowl berth, he also was an All-American in track and field. The prior season on the gridiron, he played on the famed "Hard Rocks" defense that allowed just 5.9 points per game and actually outscored their opponents 58-53. Voss could not play professionally due to a career-ending knee injury.

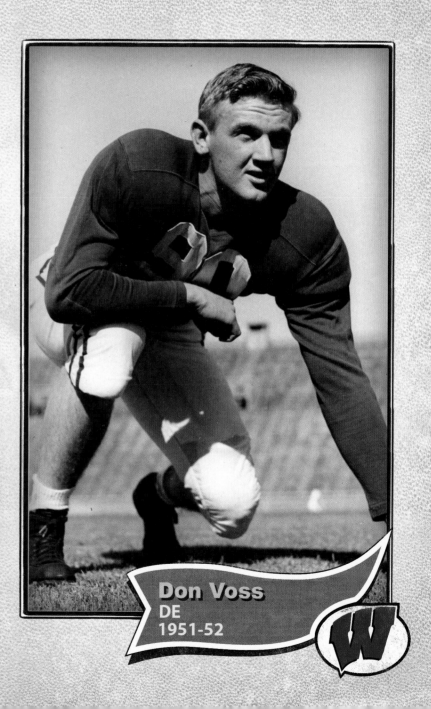

Don Voss
DE
1951-52

★ ★

★ ★ ★ ★ ★ # SEVEN ★ ★ ★ ★ ★

Seven Badgers have been tabbed as the Big Ten Player of the Year: fullback
Howard Weiss (1938), end Dave Schreiner (1942), center Robert "Red" Wilson
(1949), fullback Alan Ameche (1954), quarterback Ron Vander Kelen (1962),
and running backs Brent Moss (1993) and Ron Dayne (1999).

★ ★

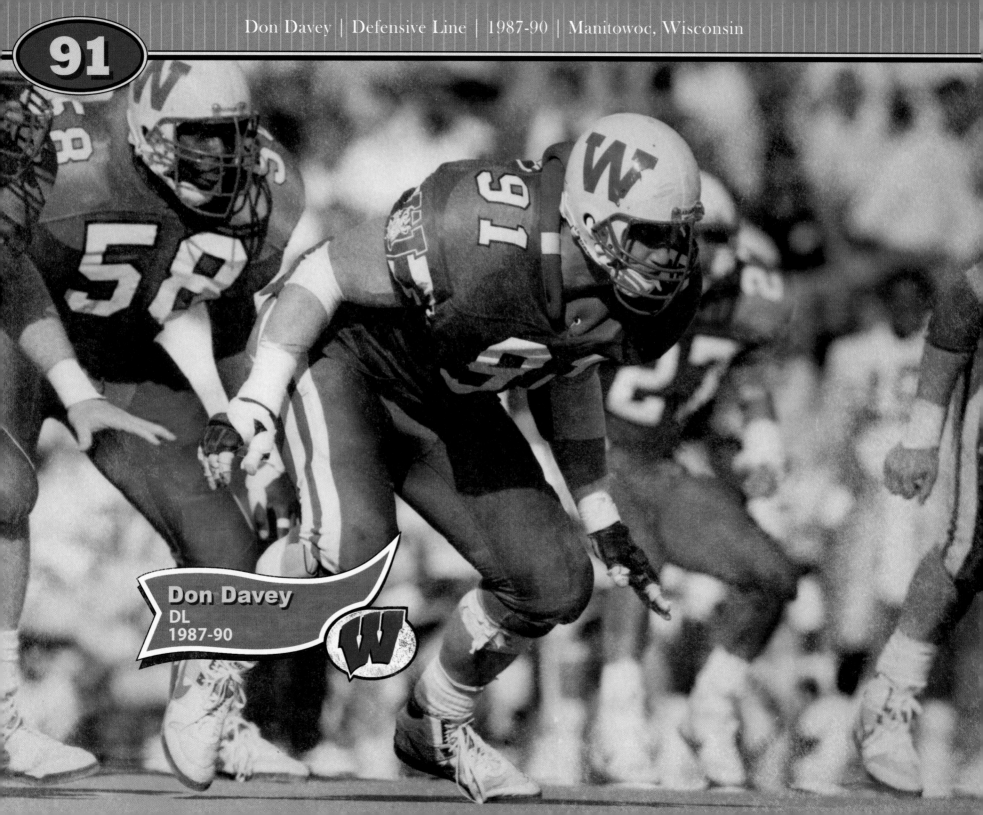

Don Davey
DL
1987-90

Nothing can match the thrill Don Davey got from chasing around quarterbacks and butting helmets with 300-pound offensive linemen.

But Davey found something that comes close: the grind of Ironman competitions.

"When you're done playing football, you just can't call your buddies and call a bunch of neighbors together and get up a game of tackle football together in the street," said Davey, who retired in 1999 after eight seasons in the NFL with the Green Bay Packers and Jacksonville Jaguars. "When it's over, it's over.

"I was very fortunate to get hooked on these triathlons."

It didn't exactly start out well for Davey, who competed in a short-distance triathlon shortly after retiring while attempting to slim down from his playing weight of 285 pounds and nearly didn't live to tell about it.

"I almost drowned," he said. "It was the worst thing I ever did in my life."

Davey viewed it as a challenge and attacked it with a vengeance, taking aim at the pinnacle of the sport, the Ironman triathlons, which consist of a 2.4-mile swim, 112-mike bike ride and are topped off by a full marathon (26.2 miles).

Davey completed Ironman events in Madison in 2005 and the United Kingdom two years later. His latest venture was Ironman Austria, which he finished in July 2009 in 11 hours, 15 minutes - topping his goal by 45 minutes.

Ultimately, he wants to qualify for the big kahuna -- Ironman Hawaii.

"The cool thing is, I'm a total fish out of water in these things," Davey said. "Even now, I'm down to about 220-225 (pounds), but I'm still the biggest guy in these races by probably 50 pounds. The fact that I can compete and compete well in these things, it really does fuel that competiveness for me."

You had to be an Ironman to survive the Don Morton era at Wisconsin. Davey played three years under Morton, who was fired following the 1989 season after compiling a 6-27 record.

That first season under new coach Barry Alvarez wasn't easy - the Badgers were 1-10 - but Alvarez still points to guys like Davey as the building blocks for the glory years that followed.

"He was the guy that I tried to explain to everyone else, 'This is how you play the game,'" Alvarez said of Davey, a first-team All-Big Ten pick and the team's MVP as a senior in 1990.

Davey was a model student as well. A mechanical engineering major, he was a four-time, first-team Academic All-American and was the subject of a *Sports Illustrated* article during his junior season despite the fact the Badgers had a 3-7 record at the time.

At the time of the *SI* article, Davey wanted to "design artificial limbs, surgical instruments and heart and lung machines" after his playing career was finished.

Instead, the Manitowoc native helped start an institutional money management firm. The company has over $100 million in assets; former and current NFL players represent about 20 percent of the firm's clients.

"I really started it as a favor to some buddies because I got sick of watching them get taken by some of these other guys," said Davey, 41, who also owns 10 restaurant franchises in the Orlando area.

Football is still a big part of Davey's life - flag football, that is.

Two of his five daughters are members of an all-girls team that Davey coaches in a previously all-boys league. The team holds its own, too.

"There's nothing that I couldn't do with my daughters that I could do if I had a son as well," said Davey, who started dating his wife, Kristen, in the ninth grade. "I feel like I'm the luckiest guy in the world."

92

Carlos Fowler
DL
1990-93

A member of Barry Alvarez's first recruiting class at UW, Fowler started 33 games during his career with the Badgers. That class helped UW win Big Ten and Rose Bowl championships during the 1993 season. Not only did Fowler help the Badgers keep other teams from scoring, he also helped UW put some points on the board by scoring two touchdowns during his career after recovering fumbles in the end zone.

Frederick Gage
QB
1938-40

Gage was a jack of all trades for the Badgers. He played fullback on the freshman team, spent two seasons as a backup quarterback, then moved to the offensive line for his final season. "Backfield men do not shift into the line to receive big headlines," *The Capital Times* wrote about Gage in 1940. "Fred Gage did. That is why the Badgers consider him a valuable man." Gage, an accomplished amateur golfer, went on to become the radio voice of the Badgers for 35 years. "There are certain people who are characters in the loveable sense of the word, and Fred was one of them," former UW athletic director Pat Richter said after Gage died in 2003.

Not too many punters are elected as team captains, but DeBauche was in 2007. Inspired by another great punter from the Green Bay area, Kevin Stemke, DeBauche finished his career at UW second only to Stemke by averaging 42.5 yards per punt. DeBauche's 44.8-yard average as a sophomore in 2005 earned him first-team All-Big Ten honors. The next season, he was named a second-team All-American by SI.com.

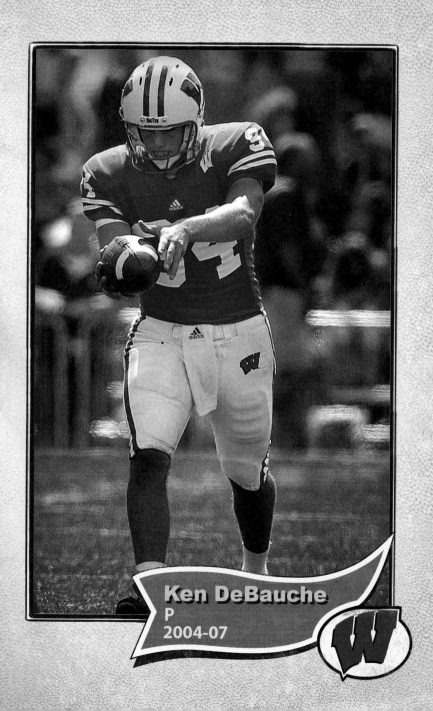

Ken DeBauche
P
2004-07

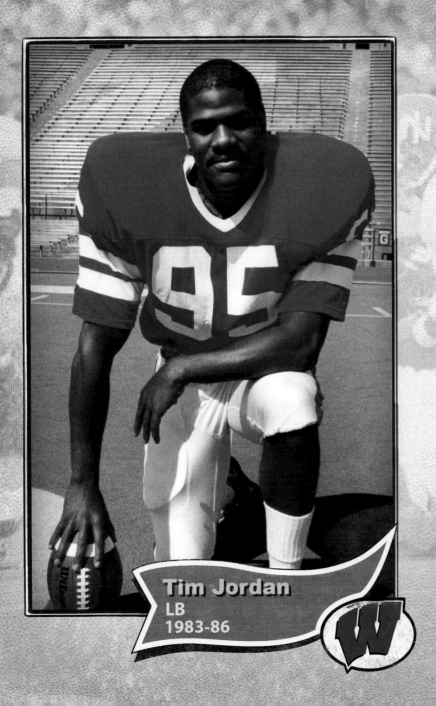

Tim Jordan
LB
1983-86

A hometown product from Madison La Follette High School, Jordan ranks fourth in UW in career sacks with 27 and served as one half of the "Thunder and Lightning" tandem with Rick Graf, who is No. 99 on our list. Jordan had six sacks in one game during a 17-14 home loss to Northwestern in 1985. A season earlier, he was named UW's Jay Seiler Coaches Appreciation winner. Jordan was selected by the New England Patriots in the fourth round in 1987 and played three seasons in the NFL.

A four-year starter and captain in 2000, Favret was a member of teams that won Big Ten and Rose Bowl titles during the 1998 and '99 seasons. UW's defense allowed the fewest points per game nationally in 1998 and ranked fifth in that category the following season. Favret, who was chronically undersized at 240 pounds, was named UW's Jay Seiler Coaches Appreciation award winner in 2000 and co-winner in 1998.

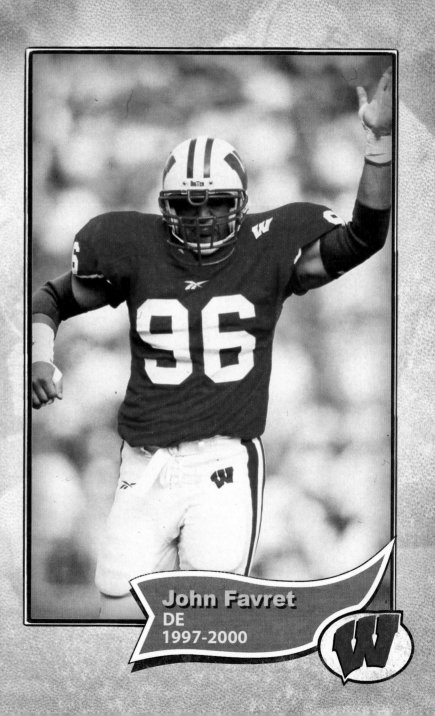

John Favret
DE
1997-2000

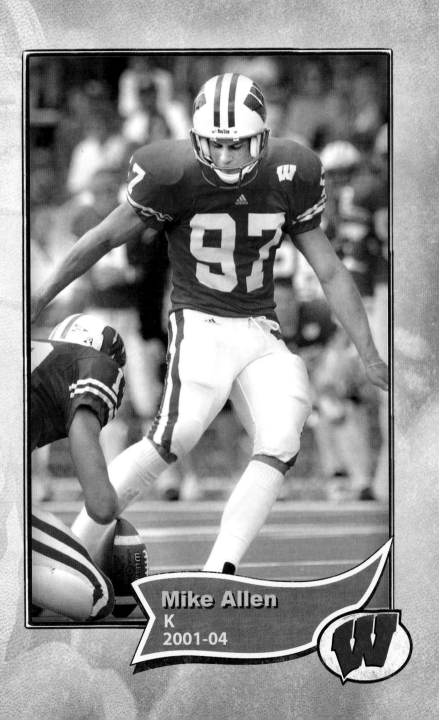

Mike Allen
K
2001-04

Before switching his number to No. 99 for his final two seasons, Allen made quite an impact wearing No. 97. He kicked two game-winning field goals during the 2002 season, a 37-yarder in overtime to beat Colorado in the Alamo Bowl and a 34-yarder with 2:05 left in a 23-21 victory over Fresno State. Allen ranks fourth all-time at UW in field goals (39) and extra points (97) and sixth in field-goal percentage (.639).

98

Burgess led the 1993 team that won Big Ten and Rose Bowl titles in tackles with 100, including 10 for loss. He also forced a team-high seven fumbles. Burgess' last game might have been one of his best; he recorded a team-high 12 tackles in UW's 21-16 victory over UCLA in the 1994 Rose Bowl.

Yusef Burgess
LB
1990-93

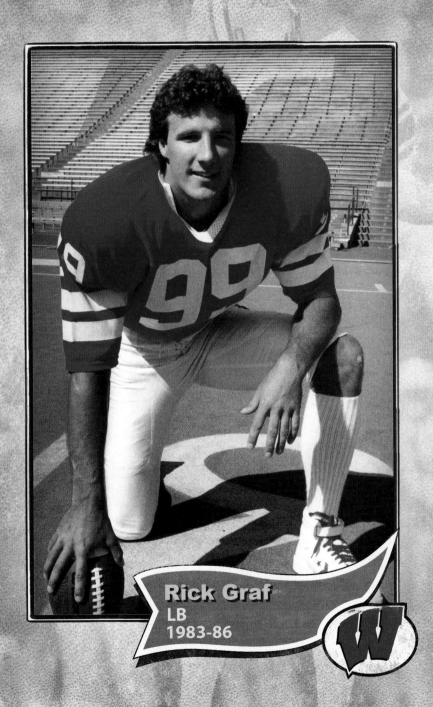

Rick Graf
LB
1983-86

A four-year starter out of Madison Memorial, Graf finished his career with six fumble recoveries, tied for third at UW. He had 11 tackles for loss as a sophomore in 1984 and overcame a torn ACL that ended his junior season. Graf was part of the famed "Thunder and Lightning" tandem with Tim Jordan, who is No. 95 on our list. Selected in the second round of the 1987 NFL Draft by the Miami Dolphins, he played seven seasons in the NFL with the Dolphins, Houston Oilers and Washington Redskins.

★ HONORABLE MENTIONS ★

1
RB John Williams (1979-82)
WR Luke Swan (2004-08)

2
WR Lee DeRamus (1991-93)
DB Scott Starks (2001-04)
RB Brian Calhoun (2005)

3
P Dick Mileager (1975-77)
DB Ken Stills (1983-84)

4
DB Bill Drummond (1973-75)
DB Jay Seiler (1978)
DB Robert Williams (1985-87)
WR Michael London (1991-95)

5
K Todd Gregoire (1984-87)

6
K Wendell Gladem (1981-83)
DB Kevin Huntley (1994-97)
DB Joey Boese (1998-01)
DB Brett Bell (2001-05)

7
DL Pat Collins (1974-76)
KS Steve Veith (1977-79)
QB Mike Howard (1984-86)
DB Eddie Fletcher (1988-91)

8
DB Ken Simmons (1973-75)
DB Greg Gordon (1975-78)

9
S Dave Fronek (1963-65)
QB Ron Miller (1960-61)
DB Clint Sims (1979-82)
WR Jonathan Orr (2002-05)

10
WR David Charles (1976-78)
DB Reggie Holt (1990-93)
K Taylor Mehlhaff (2004-07)

11
QB Darrell Bevell (1992-95)
TE Owen Daniels (2002-05)

12
QB Neil Graff (1969-71)
LB Alex Lewis (2002-03)

13
QB John Josten (1978, 80, 82)

14
P Kevin Stemke (1997-2000)

15
DB/ST Tim Rosga (1996-99)

16
DB Joe Stellmacher (2003-06)

17
DB Melvin Tucker (1990-94)

18
HB Clarence Self (1943, 46-48)
P Scott Cepicky (1984-87)
K Rich Thompson (1988-92)

19
LB Darryl Carter (1993-96)
QB Jim Sorgi (2000-03)

20
RB/WR William Yanakos (1966-68)
DL Dan Relich (1976-78)
WR Thad McFadden (1980-81
83-84)
K Vitaly Pisetsky (1997-00)

21
QB/K/P Jim Bakken (1959-61)
DB Robb Johnston (1972-74)
DB Scott Erdmann (1975-78)

22
WR Marvin Neal (1979-81; 83)
WR/ST Nick Davis (1998-01)

23
QB Larry Hanzel (1948-49)
RB/WR Randy Marks (1968-70)
TB Chucky Davis (1979-82)

24
DB Alvin Peabody (1972-74)
DB/ST Korey Manley (1990-92)

25
RB Larry Emery (1983-86)

26
P Sam Veit (1991-94)
DB Bobby Myers (1996-99)

27
HB Louis Holland (1961-63)
DB Greg Thomas (1987-90)

28
RB Anthony Davis (2001-04)
FB Dave Mohapp (1978-81)
K Matt Davenport (1997-98)

29
DB Jeff Messenger (1991-94)
LB Bob Adamov (1995-98)
RB Michael Bennett (1999-00)

30
FB Wayne Todd (1966-68)
FB Gary Lund (1970-72)

31
TE/FB Matt Nyquist (1992-95)

32
KR Greg Johnson (1969, 1971)
FB Robert Radcliffe (1948-50)
FB Ken Starch (1973-75)
FB Mark Montgomery (1990-93)

33
(Retired)
RB Brent Moss (1991-94)
LB Jim Melka (1982-84)
FB Mike Morgan (1974-77)
LB Ken Criter (1966-68)

34
OL Greg Kabat (1930-32)
RB Marvin Artley (1985-88)
LB Rick Jakious (1972-74)

35
(Retired)
Dennis Stejskal (1975-77)
Chuck Winfrey (1968-70)

36
FB T.A. Cox (1944, 46-48)
OL Mike Jenkins (1972-74)
FB Charles Green (1979-82)
DB Mike Echols (1998-01)

37
HB Roy Bellin (1936-38)
FB Alan Thompson (1969-71)
DB Lawrence Johnson (1975-78)
DB Scott Nelson (1990-93)

38
FB James Purnell (1961-63)
DB LaMarr Campbell (1994-97)

39
Walter "Mickey" McGuire (1930-32)
FB George Paskvan (1938-40)
WR Jeff Mack Sr. (1972-74)
RB P.J. Hill (2006-08)

40
(Retired)
HB Rollie Strehlow (1949-51)
HB William Smith (1961-63)
ATH Stu Voigt (1967-69)

41
HB Harland Carl (1951-53)
LB Dave Ahrens (1977-80)
RB Gary Ellerson (1982-83)
RB Terrell Fletcher (1991-94)
LB Mark Zalewski (2003-06)

★ HONORABLE MENTIONS ★

42
WR Tim Stracka (1978-80; 82)
LB Brendan Lynch (1988-91)

43
FB William Lusby (1928-30)
DB Michael Cavill (1967-68)

44
HB/LB Deral Teteak (1949-51)
RB Merritt Norvell (1960-62)
LB Dan Kissling (1986-89)
FB Chris Pressley (2005, 07-08)

45
RB Carl Silvestri (1962-64)
FB Matt Bernstein (2002-05)

46
HB Eugene "Gene" Evans (1946-49)
LS Mike Schneck (1996-98)

47
OL Rube Wagner (1926-28)
G John Parks (1927-29)
LB Dave Levenick (1977-81)
LB Eric Unverzagt (1991, 93-95)

48
E Leonard Lovshin (1933, 35-36)
LB David Wings (1985-88)
LB Aaron Norvell (1989-92)

49
DB Henry Searcy (1990-93)

50
C Dick Teteak (1956-58)
LB Chris Hein (1991-94)

51
C Fred Negus (1942, 46)

52
C Jim Moore (1976-78)
LB Michael Reid (1983-86)

53
C George Simkowski (1950-52)
LB Craig Raddatz (1983-86)
C Donovan Raiola (2002-05)

54
C Joe Kelly (1947-49)
OL Dave Costa (1997-00)
DL Mike Newkirk (2005-08)

55
LB Russ Fields (1981-85)

56
E Albert Lorenz (1938-40)
OL Brad Jackomino (1975-78)

57
LB Dave Lokanc (1970-72)
LB Gary Casper (1989-92)

58
LB Malvin Hunter (1987-90)

59
C Joe Rothbauer (1977-80)
DL Dick Teets (1982-85)

60
OL Jerry Stalcup (1957-59)
OL Bill Ferrario (1997-00)
OL Steve Lick (1975-77)
OL Steve Stark (1992-95)

61
OL Wray George (1945-47)
OL Paul Shwaiko (1952, 54-55, 58)
OL Donald Murphy (1967-69)
OL Rodney Lossow (1985-87)

62
RG Donald Knauff (1946-49)
OL George O'Brien (1950-52)
OL Keith Nosbusch (1970-72)
DL Lamark Shackerford (1990-93)

63
OL Jack Murray (1937-39)
OL Clarence Stensby (1951-54)
OL Terry Lyons (1974-76)
OL Kraig Urbik (2005-08)

64
OL George Steinmetz (1950-52)
OL Stephen Ambrose; (1954-55)
LB Mike Herrington (1979-80, 82-83)

65
OL John Simcic (1948-50)
OL Jerry Frei (1942; 46-47)
OL Marcus Coleman (2004-07)

66
OL Bob Richter (1964-66)
OL Bob Landsee (1982-83, 85)
OL William Gable (1948-49, 51)

67
OL Bob Kennedy (1950-52)
OL Mike Verstegen (1991-94)

68
OL Mark Tauscher (1997-99)

69
None

70
OL Roger Pillath (1961-63)
DL Jason Maniecki (1991, 93-95)
OL Casey Rabach (1997-00)

71
OL Jerry Wunsch (1993-96)

72
OL Bruce Elliott (1944, 47-49)
OL Jeff Dellenbach (1981-84)
OL Al Johnson (1999-02)

73
OL Lee Bernet (1962-64)

74
DL Jim Schymanski (1971-73)
OL Tom Kaltenberg (1975-77)
DL Jason Jefferson (2001-04)

75
FB Howard Weiss (1936-38)
OL Ray Snell (1977-79)
OL Chuck Belin (1989-92)

76
OL Clarence Esser (1943-46)

77
DT Anttaj Hawthorne (2001-04)

78
OL Harold "Hal" Otterback (1946-49)

79
OL Tom Domres (1965-67)
OL Bob Winckler (1979-82)

80
(Retired)
None

81
TE Mike Roan (1991-94)
TE Mark Anelli (1998-01)

82
E Ken Sachtjen (1948-50)
E David Kocourek (1956-58)

83
(Retired)
None

84
E David Howard (1954-56)
WR Melvin Reddick (1967-69)

85
E James Reinke (1954-56)
TE Ron Egloff (1973-76)
DL Curt Blaskowski (1978-80)

86
LS Matt Katula (2000-04)

HONORABLE MENTIONS

87
TE Dague Retzlaff (1996-2000)
WR Darrin Charles (2000-2004)

88
(Retired)
TE Larry Mialik (1969-71)
TE Jeff Nault (1980-83)
WR Chris Chambers (1997-2000)

89
E Kenton Peters (1951-52)
RE Henry Derleth (1958-60)
TE/DL/LB Jeff Vine (1976-79)

90
DE Erasmus James (2001-02, 04)
DL Gary Dickert (1972-74)

91
DL Jason Chapman (2004-08)

92
DE Matt Shaughnessy (2004-08)

93
None

94
DE Eric Rice (1964-66)

95
LB Guy Boliaux (1978-81)
DL Joe Monty (2003-06)

96
LB Brad Grabow (1981-84)
DL Nick Hayden (2003-07)

97
T John Heineke (1954-56)
E James Holmes (1957-58)

98
K Rick Schnetzky (1993-94)
DL Darius Jones (2001-03)

99
DL Jake Sprague (1998-02)

BEFORE THERE WERE NUMBERS

Players didn't wear numbers in the early days of college football, which means that several legendary names in University of Wisconsin history were not eligible for the All-Time Roster. Here are some players who would have been strong candidates. All were first-team All-Americans except Pat O'Dea, who is a member of the College Football Hall of Fame. The years listed are when the players earned varsity letters.

Pat O'Dea, K, 1896-99
Robert Butler, T, 1911-13
Ray Keeler, G, 1912-14
Arlie Mucks, G, 1914
Howard Buck, T, 1913-15

Paul Meyers, E, 1915-16, '19
George C. Bunge, C, 1919-21
Frank Weston, E, 1917, '19-20
Ralph Scott, T, 1917, '19-20
Marty Below, T, 1918, '22-23

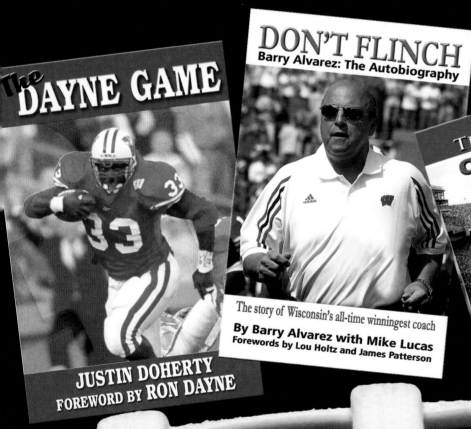
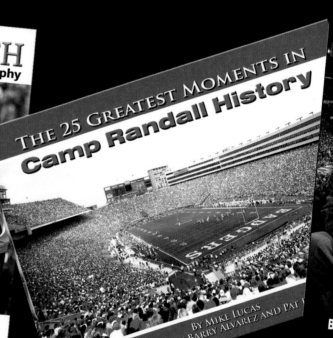